Rocko Jay Solid

Dr. Paul Saladino

On the dangers of seed oils

Featuring Interviews with Dr. Chris Knobbe
and other Linoleic Acid Experts

Revised Transcripts

25% of the royalties will go to Prof. Dr. Thomas
Seyfrieds cancer research!

*P.S.: Any review would be GREATLY appreciated to get
the Low-Carb message out!*

TABLE OF CONTENTS

Chapter 1
The dangers of banning my post on seed oils

We are in an environment where bucking the norm or talking about things that are outside of the mainstream is not tolerated, and that is very dangerous!

On this week's podcast, I'm pushing back directly against claims that some of the things I've said about seed oils on instagram are misinformation.

If you follow me on Instagram, you may have seen one of the reels that I posted there, about how canola oil is made. In which I say that seed oils like canola oil appear to be pretty harmful for humans.

This got flagged by Instagram as *partial misinformation*, which means that Instagram stops promoting that reel... which had been seen over 3.5 million times and was certainly getting a lot of people thinking, getting them curious. But Instagram says **No** because the ‚independent fact checkers' are saying *it's misinformation.*

So I'm going to look at the independent fact checker article this week and dismantle it, piece by piece, showing you guys clear evidence that seed oils are in fact harmful for humans. That canola oil is from a rape plant which has been hybridized to be low erucic acid.

This type of censorship is a very dangerous thing for our health environment. Who gets to decide what is medical misinformation? When did it become a state of affairs that if you differ from the mainstream medical perspective, you are deemed *misinformation?* Your content is censored, your content is shadowbanned and demoted and no one sees that. How can we have discourse about different ideas if that becomes the case? And who do we select as the one all-knowing expert that gets to decide what the misinformation is?

As you'll read in this podcast, there's a researcher at Tufts that I take pretty significant issue with. This is the same guy who's behind the Food Compass Guidelines, that have recently rated Fruit Loops, Cheerios and Honey Nut Cheerios above things like ground beef and eggs cooked in butter for nutritional health!

Clearly, this guy is living in an upside-down world. Well, he's one of the people they reference in the AFP fact checker article as an expert, saying that *seed oils are not harmful for humans at all* - and citing my reel as misinformation.

So buckle up for a seed oil food fight! Obviously, I've tried to be respectful in this episode as I always try to be. But I'm going to show you lots of information that seed oils are in fact harmful for humans and that I disagree with this individual's research about seed oils vehemently.

And: You should definitely eliminate seed oils from your diet!

The broader point here is that this type of censorship, this type of labeling of misinformation, is very dangerous in the medical world. If we are to have interesting discourse about different ideas, and if we are ever going to really find the truth about how humans, how you, how someone else could really be healthy - this is really important.

Who gets to decide what is misinformation!

This is becoming a really important question. And it was made even more relevant to me last week, when one of my reels on Instagram was tagged as *partly false*. So it got me thinking *who decides that this reel is partly false misinformation*?

It wasn't about any viral things, it was about seed oils. In the video, I was showing canola oil, I was talking about how it was made and I was saying that seed oils are harmful for humans.

I want to go through the AFP fact checker article that they reference, when they say it's misinformation.

And I'm going to go to systematically address all of the claims they make in that article and talk about why I think they're full of sh*t - and why this is a very dangerous slippery slope!

You guys have heard me talk about seed oils many times, but I'm going to recapitulate much of that. I'm going to talk about some of the most compelling studies. I'm not going to do a total breakdown about seed oils in this podcast, but I'm going to talk about some of the most compelling studies, showing that seed oils look to be very harmful for humans.

A third party saying that seed oils are not harmful is essentially muzzling me, censoring information... open discussion on those social media platforms allows for proper respectful discourse. This is how we all learn. If it gets to a point on social media, whether it's Instagram, Twitter, YouTube or wherever...

Where we are only allowed to talk about medical information or nutritional information in a way that aligns with the mainstream narrative - we have come to a very, very dark place! And getting a reel on Instagram talking about seed oils labeled as partly false is dangerous. I think that it's a step in that direction.

Who gets to decide?

So let's dig in and I will talk about seed oils:

- I'll talk about how they're harmful
- I'll talk about evidence that corroborates everything I said in that video on Instagram, and
- I will talk about why the claims that are being noted in the fact checker article aren't actually true.

In the fact checker article, they're referencing a few people as their ‚experts‘ who say that seed oils are beneficial for humans - and I will talk about studies that those people have done.

I'm referring specifically to Dariush Mozaffarian, he is the Dean of Nutrition at Tufts University School of Nutrition, and he along with Walter Willett and Frank Hugh are really the biggest voices in the nutrition space now.

Because Frank Hugh and Walter Willet are at Harvard, and Dariush Mozaffarian is at Tufts - and these guys are essentially making nutrition policy.

A lot of the studies that they're connected with are funded by Unilever, which used to be the single greatest purveyor of seed oils in the country. These guys tend to have a partyline, they tend to be on a plant-based / vegan line. And so many of the studies they're doing are excluding important studies that might be contradictory to the point they're trying to prove.

I will show you a 2009 meta-analysis of randomized controlled trials, looking at polyunsaturated fatty acids (PUFAs) done by Darius Mazafarian, which excludes the randomized controlled trials done in the 60s and 70s, specifically the Minnesota Coronary Study and Sydney Diet Heart Study - which found that seed oils were harmful for humans!

There is this perspective in nutritional science, that says: We need to go by this pyramid of evidence.

There is a hierarchy of evidence, and meta-analyzes of randomized controlled trials are the gold standard... except when the person doing the meta-analysis can conveniently exclude trials whose conclusions go against their party line!

The overarching message is that we all need to be humble. We're learning. And open debate, open discussion, open respectful discussion is how we all learn. If that goes away, we're in a very dangerous place.

I hope that these important nutritional conversations with conflicting views can continue to happen, because they are nuanced and it is dangerous for platforms like Instagram or any other platform to say *this is partly false based on...* what?

So this is the reel [Showing the video with audio in the podcast]

> *Canola oil is toxic! Here's how it's made: It starts with the seeds of a rape plant, which are completely toxic to humans in order to make canola oil.*

This is true, the seeds of a rape plant are toxic to humans. They have to be lowered in erucic acid.

> *These plants must be specially bred to lower the levels of erucic acid, a toxic fatty acid strongly associated with heart lesions. These seeds are then ground at high temperatures to extract the fragile oil, which is inevitably oxidized because of this harsh process.*

Nothing crazy so far. You take rape seeds from a low erucic acid canola plant...

The name CANOLA is an acronym for Canadian Oil Low Acid, there's no such thing as a canola plant. That was made up by the Canola Association a few decades ago, when they took these rape seed plants and decided to make them into an oil.

Previously, these type of things were used as machine lubricants! Canola is not a plant, rape seeds are a plant. But that plant has never been food for humans!

You must genetically breed that plant to have lower levels of a monounsaturated fatty acid called erucic acid, which is pretty strongly correlated with harmful heart lesions. 6

Look up Keshen's Disease in humans!

So canola is a special variety of rapeseed with low erucic acid, erucic acid being a harmful thing for humans. If we have to take erucic acid out of a plant, why are we making oil out of that plant in the first place? And when you grind it up and heat it, it's going to become oxidized.

I will show you evidence that canola oil contains between 1.9 and 3.6% trans fatty acids, which are formed in the process of heating and hydrogenation and oxidation. This is a pretty significant level! As I've spoken about on social media: When oils like canola or soybean oil say *0 trans fat*, that is not true! Manufacturers can technically say that if they have less than 0.5 grams of trans fat *per serving*. Well, a serving of oil is usually only 14 grams. A tablespoon. Maybe even a teaspoon!

So if there's less than 0.5 grams per 14 grams [3.5%], then they can say it's 0 trans fat! But if the oil is 1.9 to 3.6% trans fatty acids, they're actually getting pretty close to that threshold, though they're not exceeding it. But do you want to eat an oil that's 1.9 to 3.6% trans fatty acids? Definitely not, if those are trans fatty acids from vegetables.

I'll say there are trans fatty acids in animal foods, conjugated linoleic acid, a completely different trans fat than you will find when linoleic acid becomes a trans fat in the heating process.

So conjugated linoleic acid is a different fatty acid, depends on where the trans hydrogen atoms are in the molecule. Conjugated linoleic acid and other trans fatty acids in animal foods have actually been associated with health improvements. While we know very clearly...

I don't think anyone would debate this, and: In fact, Ansel Keys himself was the one who discovered that trans fatty acids raise LDL. And further research - not necessarily by him, but by others – clearly, strongly associated trans fatty acids from vegetables and plant oils with severely bad health outcomes.

It appears that trans fatty acids formed from the hydrogenation, the heating of polyunsaturated vegetable oils, inhibit process cyclings and promote thromboxane in the clotting process. Being pro-clotting and antithrombolytics, making it more likely that you will clot. Well, that sounds like a bad thing!

So let's continue on this reel:

> *This oil must then be washed with solvents like hexane, a known neurological toxin.*

Hexane is a neurological toxin! It appears that the amount of hexane in canola oil is about 8 parts per million[ppm]. Now, it's debatable whether this amount is something that is going to impact humans negatively. But do you want you, your kids or your family ingesting significant known amounts of hexane, a known neurological toxin? If you can avoid it?

There are so many toxins we come in contact in our environment, that we can't avoid, why would you knowingly eat an oil that is refined, bleached and deodorized - and all the seed oils are like this, whether it's canola or soybean or any of these oils - that has hexane?

And we can debate all day, back and forth whether that's a significant amount of hexane. But I don't want any excess hexane in my diet! Then it must be processed with bleaching and deodorization so it doesn't smell rancid. Like it really is.

> *After all of these steps, the canola oil is left oxidized, contaminated with solvents and containing significant levels of trans fatty acids.*

I'm going to show you evidence later that the significant levels of trans fatty acids in canola oil are 1.9 to 3.6%, that's a significant amount of trans fatty acids.

> *And this oil is marketed to you as healthy by the American Heart Association, and is found in so many of our foodstuffs today.*

That's true, the American Heart Association gives canola oil its little check mark which is essentially the American Heart Association's seal of approval.

Manufacturers must pay for that - which is a whole different discussion and a whole different bag of worms... about the corruption with AHA and the millions of dollars that they have gained by putting these heart labels on foods.

And who decides what's heart healthy? I don't know, if it lowers LDL, it's heart healthy. Even if in lowering that LDL, it increases death! Like the Minnesota Coronary study found, Or even if it increases things like oxidized LDL and LP(a).

> *If you want to be healthy, get this damaged oil out of your diet completely!*

As you can see at the bottom of the video, it says *this is partly false information*. We are going to factcheck the factcheckers.

So that was the reel - and again, who gets to decide that anything I said in there was misinformation?

The *how canola oil is made* reel was one of the best performing reels I had put out in many months. It had over 3.7 million views and over 90,000 likes! I think there were thousands of comments on that reel.

When the factchecker put on a factcheck notice on there, Instagram probably stops promoting it completely and no one is going to see that anymore.

So what I believe was very valuable information about the damages of canola oil, Instagram says „Nope, no one else is going to see this" - and that is a very dangerous thing. So let's go to the actual AFP.

I guess AFP is an organization that does fact checking. The fact check article that they used to put the misinformation label on my Instagram post.

Here's the AFP fact checker article: They say „*Posts mislead on the health effects of seed oils*", so let's see, shall we?

[URL: https://factcheck.afp.com/doc.afp.com.333B473] (1)

This is written by Rob Lever, I have no idea who that is, so I will read this:

> *Blogs and social media posts claim many vegetable oils, such as those made from sunflower and canola, can promote inflammation that leads to heart disease and other ailments.*
> *This is misleading...*

according to AFP factcheck.

I will show you multiple peer-reviewed randomized controlled trials that show that seed oils do some really nasty things, like increasing lipid peroxidation, oxidized LDL, LP(a) and Lp-PLA2.

I don't think any cardiologist on the planet would argue that if you're ingesting those things, that that is going to lead to heart disease. So who's fact checking the factchecker here?

Regardless, AFP factcheck says this is misleading.

> *Health experts...*

...I don't know... Well, I do know what health experts they're talking about, we'll get back into Dariush Mozaffarian later.

> *Health experts say consumption of seed oils can be beneficial, if not included in highly processed foods.*

I'm not exactly sure how highly processed foods versus non-highly processed foods is going to change the way seed oils work in your body. Also, considering that seed oils themselves are highly processed!

I don't know, you can put seed oils into a highly processed food. But, what's a highly processed food? Are potato chips highly processed? What about saute at your local restaurant, cooked in seed oils, that's not bad for you? But potato chips are? They're using the same seed oils.

What about a salad dressing with seed oil, is that highly processed? I think this is kind of hand waving voodoo to hedge their bets and say „Oh, seed oils are fine for you, if they're not in highly processed foods."

> "The consumption of vegetable oils (seed oils) has jumped along with the rates of chronic illness, infertility & obesity," says a November 30, 2022 Instagram post.

That's not my post, but that is in fact an association, that is a true thing.

> In an Instagram video published November 25th, the narrator says:
> „These vegetable oils, also called seed oils, they get stuck in your cell membranes in body fat for 2 to 5 years." Similar claims were made on Tick Tock.

I don't know if these factcheckers are debating the claim that seed oils get stuck in our cell membranes for 2 to 5 years, or if they're just saying that people are stating that online.

But: The best evidence we have regarding the pharmacokinetics of polyunsaturated fatty acids suggests that their half-life is 680 days. Well, it takes 4.5 half-lives to get rid of something, if you've taken pharmacology.... That's a pretty significant amount of time!

That sounds like about those 2 to 5 years that a molecule of linoleic acid could get stuck in your cell membrane.

One thing that is not debatable is that polyunsaturated fatty acids gets stored in your body. Your body can interconvert saturated monounsaturated fats, so we can get rid of saturated or monosaturated fatty acids and shift. But we can't get rid of polyunsaturated fats through any sort of enzymatic process!

They are stored in your body and then slowly get removed from the cell membranes based on the flux of fats that you're taking into your body. So papers regarding the half-life of polyunsaturated fats in the human body are few and far between, but this is the best one I could find:

> Composition of lipids in human serum and adipose tissue during prolonged feeding of a diet high in unsaturated fat. (2)

I quote this study from 1966, page 1:

> *Adipose tissue linoleic acid rose in men on the experimental diet from 11% of initital fatty acids at time zero, to 32% at 5 years. The rise could be fitted to an exponential function with a half-time of 680 days.*

This is probably the best and one of the only pieces of evidence we have looking at the actual pharmacokinetics of polyunsaturated fatty acids - and it says exactly what the person was saying on TikTok or Instagram, that the factchecker article seems to be dubious of.
(...)
Going back to the factchecker article. They're saying

> *The post references comments from physician Cate Shanahan...*

Sure, I think that Cate's work is great and probably based on science. They say

> *Some posts have linked seed oils to an array of diseases and ailments, including cancer, diabetes, asthma and arthritis.*

I think that these are definitely *linked* to these diseases! That is a term that's used very often in medical science. Linked means associated – so that is a true statement.

You can find many studies that link the consumption of seed oils to these things. And: The temporal association of increased seed oil consumption with a significant rise in obesity, asthma, diabetes, chronic illness is real.
 So you can't really argue that seed oils appear to be linked to these things.

> *Other posts recommend replacing seed oils with animal fats or other plant oils.*

Well, that's absolutely true and I think that that's totally reasonable.

This AFP fact checker article seems to be insinuating in some way, that replacing seed oils with animal fats could never be good for humans. In fact, that's the position I would take in total - that it's much

11

better to replace seed oils with animal fats, which are much lower in linoleic acid.

So here's where things are about to get interesting:

> *Medical experts say all fats are high in calories and should be consumed in moderation, but claims that vegetable and seed oils are harmful are misleading.*

I'm not sure how these posts are misleading and I will corroborate that statement: Let's just talk about some pretty significant evidence that seed oils are harmful for humans.

Again, the framework of this whole conversation is the concern that:

Just because the people who wrote this fact checker article decided to talk to Dariush Mozaffarian, and he says that seed oils are beneficial for humans and these claims are misleading, they are! And we don't get to have any discussion about it.

Instagram will censor the post, stop promoting it and we don't have any ability to have discussions about contentious or interesting topics on Instagram.

I will issue a slight warning, we're about to get kind of technical. I'm going to show a bunch of articles, but this is my assertion that there is plenty of evidence that seed oils are going to increase your risk of cardiovascular disease.

Let's start with this study first, the title is

Effects of an oleate-rich and linoleate-rich diet on the susceptibility of low density lipoprotein to oxidative modification in mildly hyper-cholesterolemic subjects. (3)

Basically, they're saying:

- We're either going to feed people olive oil, oils that are high in oleic acid. Or
- We're going to feed them seed oils, high in linoleic acid and see how fragile their LDL is. See how susceptible to oxidation their LDL particle is.

It is pretty well established within cardiovascular medicine in general, that if your LDL is oxidized, that is a major risk factor - perhaps causative of atherosclerosis in the atherosclerotic process! Macrophages don't take up native LDL, they only ingest oxidized LDL in the sub endothelial space. So having oxidized LDL is bad, having LDL that is more likely to be oxidized is really bad.

This was an 8 week diet and what they found is noted here - that LDL oxidation is altered by adding polyunsaturated fats.

> *Substitution of monounsaturated (rather than polyunsaturated) fatty acids for saturated fatty acids in the diet might be preferable for the prevention of atherosclerosis.*

Meaning that, as you see here,

> *LDL isolated from subjects on oleate-enriched diets was **less susceptible** to copper mediated oxidation, as measured by conjugated diene and lipid peroxidation formation,*
> *and **less susceptible** to LDL-protein modification, as evidenced by reduced LDL macrophage degradation after copper- or endothelial cell induced oxidation.*

So: When you give people more polyunsaturated fats, their LDL is more likely to be oxidized, both in vitro and in vivo models. And there are so many studies which continue to show the same thing.

How about another one?

> *Changes in dietary fat intake alter plasma levels of oxidized LDL and LP(a).*

LP(a) is a very known strong risk factor for cardiovascular disease. In this study, 37 healthy women were fed two diets: The saturated fat intake was decreased and the amount of polyunsaturated fat was increased. What did they find?

The amount of oxidized LDL in the plasma went up, when you do that. When you have less saturated fat and more polyunsaturated fats, the oxidized LDL goes up! So the median plasma oxidized LDL increased by 27% in response to the low-fat, low-vegetable diet - and 19% in response to the low-fat, highvegetable diet.

Also the LP(a) concentration was increased by 7% and 9%, respectively. So solid evidence that increasing polyunsaturated fat, lowering saturated fat causes more oxidized LDL.

Yet another one:

Dietary intakes of polyunsaturated fatty acids and indices of oxidative stress in human volunteers. (4)

This is a four-week study, 10 healthy non-smoking male volunteers.

The study indicates that although dietary levels of polyunsaturated fatty acids may favorably alter cholesterol profiles.

Meaning that... we know that polyunsaturated fats lower cholesterol - which isn't a good thing! See the Minnesota Coronary study, as I'll talk about later.

The same dietary changes may adversely affect some indices of lipid peroxidation. Care should be taken when providing dietary advice on PUFA intake and adequate intake of antioxidants to match any increased PUFA may be important for preventing oxidative stress.

Dear factcheckers, how are polyunsaturated fatty acids healthy for humans? Let's keep going.

Impact of 8-week linoleic acid intake in soy oil on Lp-PLA2 activity in healthy adults. (5)

Lp-PLA2 is lipoprotein-phospholipase A2, and is generally regarded as an indicator of endothelial inflammation, endothelial damage, endothelial remodeling. When you see something raise Lp-PLA2, it's not a good thing - and you can guess what happened in this study:

An increase in plasma linoleic acid following intake of soybean oil was independently associated with Lp-PLA2 activity, which was also related to apoB, ox-LDL and CEPI-CT, which is collagen.

So yet another study says that soybean oil is pretty bad, just given to people, not in processed foods! Soybean oil, given to people increases the CEPI-CT which is a indicator of endothelial function. Meaning it's getting worse. You're getting more oxidized LDL. And you're getting an increase in Lp-PLA2, which cannot possibly be a good thing.

But wait there's more:

14

The effects of diets rich in monounsaturated fatty acids on plasma lipoproteins - the Jerusalem Nutrition STUDY: High MUFAs (monounsaturated fatty acids) versus high PUFAs (polyunsaturated fatty acids). (6)

It's 26 students, randomly assigned to a 24-week crossover study. Again, all of the studies I show you are randomized controlled studies.

There was a significantly higher tendency toward lipid peroxidation on the PUFA diet, as ascertained by more thiobarbituric acid-reactive substances formations on that diet.

Dietary PUFA results in somewhat lower total cholesterol and LDL-C... no surprise there, we've seen that many times.

...where as with the monounsaturated fat the susceptibility of LDL to oxidative stress is lower.

Let's recall the whole point of that little excursion:
‚Experts' say that seed oils that are not in processed foods are healthy. And at the beginning of the AFP factchecker article they disregard the notion that seed oils are connected with heart disease. Right here:

Blog and social media posts claim many vegetable oils, such as those from sunflower and canola, can promote inflammation that leads to heart disease and other ailments.

Yeah, I would say that oxidized LDL, LP(a) thiobarbituric acid and all of these other molecules are in some ways inflammatory and promote heart disease.

Before we go any further, I just want to address the idea that seed oils lower LDL. If you're curious about LDL, listen to the many podcasts I've done on low density lipoprotein.

LDL by itself is a horrible metric as a predictor of cardiovascular disease, and we know that oxidized LDL, LP(a) are much, much better metrics. LDL by itself is a very poor predictor of cardiovascular disease!

There is a model called the homeoviscous model, in which having more polyunsaturated fatty acids in the human body probably changes the structure of the membrane, leading to lower amounts of cholesterol in the blood.

Conversely: Having more saturated fat in your diet means more saturated fats in your membranes. And remember that saturated fats are going to populate phospholipids with two straight tails, while a polyunsaturated fat will populate a phospholipid with a non-straight tail, which makes the membrane more fluid.

In a saturated fat rich diet - according to the homeopiscus model - there's probably going to be more cholesterol in the blood because of the body's intention to keep the membrane at the same level of fluidity, so that your cells are not too stiff and they're not too jelly and they don't fall apart.

So there are many physiologic reasons, that are not pathological, by which eating more saturated fat and less polyunsaturated fat may raise your LDL.

But to say that that is increasing your risk of cardiovascular disease is kind of frustrating. Because as I've shown many times, there are much better predictors of cardiovascular disease - and LDL by itself is horrible!

What about your fasting insulin? What about your fasting blood glucose? What about your glycemic excursions or your glucose variability? What about your hsCRP? What about all sorts of other inflammatory metrics?

These are much better predictors than simply looking at LDL. Which by itself is, again, a very poor predictor. Because someone with a slightly higher LDL, who is insulin sensitive, does not increase their risk of cardiovascular disease. This has been shown many times.

That, if you look at people who have moderately elevated LDL, along with moderately elevated HDL and low triglycerides, that *LDL does not have any correlation with higher rates of cardiovascular disease*. Or the correlation is significantly attenuated.

I've spoken about this at length, LDL means nothing outside of context. I have people, that send me their lipids and say „My LDL went up!" - and I say „I don't care! What's your fasting insulin?"

If you're eating more saturated fat and less polyunsaturated fat, your LDL very well may go up. But you're likely going to be much more insulin sensitive. That is where I think mainstream medicine misses the boat.

I've talked about a number of complicated lipid parameters. I want to backtrack and make sure everyone understands. The first thing that I want to point out is shown in this study, which is perhaps one of the most important points.

Binding sites on macrophages that mediates uptake and degrada-
tion of acetylated low density lipoprotein, producing
massive cholesterol deposition. (7)

It's a complicated study. What does it say?

It says that if you give a macrophage a native LDL molecule...

The macrophage is an immune cell that resides below the endo-thelium inside of your blood vessels. It is responsible for the begin-ning histopathology of an endothelial lesion or a fatty streak, **lead-ing to atherosclerosis.**

LDL is a low density lipo protein molecule, which is a phospholipid monolayer that has proteins on the outside. So imagine a balloon with proteins stuck in the membrane. LDL is like a bus, moving tri-glycerides and cholesterol around inyour body.

If you give a macrophage that native LDL, the macrophage will not take that LDL up. **That LDL must be oxidized** to be taken up by the macrophage! That is what I showed you with all those studies:

When you eat more linoleic acid, your LDL is much more likely to become oxidized!

Do we think that could be an increased risk of cardiovascular dis-ease? Is there any real cogent argument we could make, by which that would *not* be an increased risk of cardiovascular disease? I'll let you guys decide.

That is exactly, what this last paper was talking about, the one by Goldstein and others: They show that only oxidized LDL gets taken up by the macrophages.

Let's keep going, talking about oxidized LDL. Here's another study:

> *Plasma oxidized low-density lipoprotein, a strong predictor of*
> *acute coronary heart disease events in apparently healthy,*
> *middle-aged men from the general population. (8)*

From the conclusions:

> *Elevated concentrations of oxLDL are predictive of future cor-*
> *onary heart disease events in apparently healthy men. Thus,*
> *oxidized LDL may represent a promising risk marker for clini-*
> *cal coronary heart disease complications and should be evalu-*
> *ated in further studies.*

If you want to measure your oxidized LDL, what I would recommend is talking to your doctor and having them order a test through a company called Boston Heart. This is the only company that I'm aware of that does the test.

It's called <u>oxidized phospholipids on apoB.</u>

A regular oxidized LDL test is not a good test for oxidized LDL because it is a boolean assay. It is using a monoclonal antibody. Which, if it sees one or two phospholipids on the LDL and they're oxidized, it will come up as positive. Boolean means one or zero, it means true or false.

Oxidized phospholipids on apoB from Boston Heart gives you a much more accurate assay of the percentage of the phospholipids on any LDL particle that are oxidized.

I would love to do a study with this, although I don't know if an IRB would approve it (Institutional Review Board):

But I'd have two groups of people and take their LDL oxidized phospholipids apoB at baseline.

- Give one group saturated fat,
- Give one group linoleic acid containing seed oils and see what happens at the end of the trial.

We probably will do something like this in the future, through the Animal-Based Nutrition Research Foundation. It's a non-profit that I founded, because I want to do some of these studies.

It's hard to build a non-profit, we're working on funding. You can find us at abnrf.org if you want to check it out. Stay tuned for more research from the abnrf, but that's potentially in the works in the future.

But I think that doing a study like that would be very interesting, to compare saturated fat feeding (changing no other variables) versus seed oil feeding - and looking at oxidized LDL in real time in these people.

If you're interested in LP(a), here's a great paper:

> *Low-density lipoprotein cholesterol corrected for LP(a) cholesterol, risk thresholds, and cardiovascular events. (9)*

The conclusions are:

> *LDL-C was associated with incident cardiovascular disease **only** when LP(a) cholesterol content was included in the measurement.*

So they're saying that if you correct LDL for LP(a), it's not a risk factor for cardiovascular disease anymore!

What is LP(a)? It's essentially a marker of oxidized LDL, more or less. It's a little more complicated, but LP(a) appears to be a subfraction of LDL with a little protein on it that mops up oxidized lipids.

It's complicated, we don't fully understand it. But: When you correct LDL for LP(a), the risk goes away. LP(a) is a huge risk for incident cardiovascular disease! And what did I show you guys?

I showed you multiple studies, that show that lipid peroxidation increases. And a study that specifically measured LP(a) with increased polyunsaturated fats and lowering saturated fats. And what happened? LP(a) went up!

Do we really think that seed oils are not harmful? And yet, this is what is happening with factcheckers. They are independent, but are consulting experts that we'll get to in a moment. (...)

Min 36:10

Let me just say a few more things in conclusion that I think are really important - and then talk a little bit about some of the people who appear to be behind advancing the narrative that seed oils are helpful in humans. And why the research that they've published may not be something to take without careful consideration.

Let's go back to the AFP fact checker article. They say

> *Canola oil is a variety of rapeseed oil developed in Canada with low levels of erucic acid.*

That's true. I don't know why you'd want to eat oil from a plant that you have to lower the erucic acid from in the first place, but who knows.

> *In 2018, the FDA allowed the manufacturer of canola, sunflower and olive oil to make the qualified health claim that „consuming oleic acid and edible oils may reduce the risk of coronary heart disease.“*

Considering that sunflower oil is over 50% linoleic acid, I'm not sure how they get away with making a claim that oleic acid is beneficial.

And I think that oleic acid has really only been shown to be beneficial when it's substituted for polyunsaturated fats. You're always going to get oleic acid in animal fat, so don't worry about that one.

Seed oil risks are exaggerated says the AFP factcheck. Well, I think that there's a significant amount of evidence to say that they are harmful for humans.

The AFP fact checking saying *they're exaggerated* means, that the AFE factcheck says there's maybe some risk.

> *Health experts say most commercially available seed oils can be beneficial if they're not consumed as part of a highly processed packaged food and snacks.*

Again, I don't know why that has any bearing on this. Because they're going to be processed, no matter what you do.

> *A 2009 study in the journal Circulation found that people who consume between 5 and 10% of their caloric intake from polyunsaturated fatty acids - the main element of seed oils - had a lower risk of cardiovascular disease.*

Oh did it? Let's look at that 2009 study from Circulation. As you'll see here, yes, Dariush Mozaffarian is the first author in the study. They quote him saying

> *Seed oils come from nuts, seeds and beans, which are some of the healthiest foods on the planet. When humans eat these oils, their risk factors get better. They have fewer heart attacks, they have less weight gain, they are healthier than those who use other kinds of cooking fats.*

He added that

> *While industrial processing destroys some of the beneficial properties of seed oils...*

I'm not sure what the *beneficial properties* of seed oils are...

> *...that doesn't mean they're unhealthy, it means they would be healthier otherwise.*

That sounds like hand waving voodoo to me. I want to talk about for a minute about Dariush Mozaffarian: I don't like to call people out, unless it's egregious! And I think in this case, it is egregious and we have to talk about it.

If you want to know who this guy is, again, he's a Tufts. He's the chair of nutrition there and he was behind the 2018 Food Compass Guidelines.

If you guys are not familiar with these, look these up. These ranked foods, according to a metric. Looking at the overall quality of the food and the nutritional promoting qualities.

On the Food Compass Guidelines - chaired by this guy - Frosted Mini Wheats were at the top!! They were not actually the the best food, but they were pretty high! They were far above things like an egg cooked in butter and ground beef.

Anyone that devises a system that is going to rank Frosted Mini Wheats, Cheerios, Honey Nut Cheerios... an egg substitute with seed oils **above**

- a real egg cooked in butter, and
- ground beef. Not just above them, but *far* above then we have massive differences in the way we see the nutrition landscape.

Those type of conversations need to happen! Those conversations need to not be swept under the rug with a pithy *partly false misinformation* tag on Instagram.

We need to have some serious conversations with people who believe this and ask them in a respectful way how they can make claims that seed oils are healthy for humans, in light of all the evidence here, which is just the tip of the iceberg.

Let's look at the 2009 paper cited in the fact checker article and another 2009 paper from Dariush Mozaffarian, stating that seed oils are beneficial for humans.

Let's start with this one:

> *Effects on coronary heart disease of increasing polyunsaturated fat in place of saturated fat. A systematic review of and meta-analysis of randomized controlled trials.* (10)

This looks like a good title until you realize that what he's done is conflate omega-3 with omega-6! So he's lumped studies looking at omega-3 fats with omega-6 fats - which are totally different fats in human physiology.

So right from the get-go, you have something that is quite misleading, regarding polyunsaturated fat and the distinction between omega-3 and omega-6.

There are some studies that show that omega-3 fats are helpful for humans. There are also studies suggesting that long-term supplementation with fish oil leads to increased rates of cancer.

And potentially, there are also studies suggesting that long-term supplementation with omega-3 fatty acids leads to significantly increased rates of atrial fibrillation and other cardiac arrhythmias. But I'm not going to do a podcast omega-3s right now. I just want to point out that in this study... which is often cited as *suggesting / corroborating/* the *notion* that seed oils are healthy for humans:

They're conflating omega-3 with omega-6, including many trials in their analysis that are omega-3 rather than omega-6. Furthermore, if you look at the list of excluded studies from this meta-analysis...

Conveniently, Dariush Mozaffarian and his group have excluded randomized controlled trials from the 60s and 70s. Specifically, the

Minnesota Coronary Trial and the Sidney Diet Heart Trial, which showed worsening rates of coronary artery disease, coronary events and death when you had more seed oils in the diet.

As you'll see from the second article in Circulation, there gets to be a lot of argument about which trials are valid regarding randomized controlled trials for seed oils and which trials are invalid.

But: There do exist randomized controlled trials that are well done, from the 60s and 70s - showing that increased rates of consumption of seed oils lead to worsening death in the Minnesota Coronary Trial, and worsening rates of coronary artery disease in Sidney Diet Heart.

Those are conveniently left out of Darius Mazzafarian's metaanalysis of randomized controlled trials. If you would like to see the trials excluded from his meta-analysis, you can find this list of the 46 excluded trials in the supplemented materials for his 2009 paper. But in this are included the original Sidney Diet Heart and Minnesota Coronary Trial.

Now, what's interesting is: After that paper in 2009 was published – again, both of the papers here are published in 2009, there's been nothing published since then - Chris Ramsden at the NIH published two papers with reanalysis of the data from Sidney Diet Heart and the Minnesota Coronary Trial.

And these are really important to not ignore! Because as Chris says, in these trials the re-analysis doesn't look very good.

If you don't know the story: Ancel Keys was part of the Minnesota Coronary experiment team, but his name was not included on the findings because they didn't support his ideology. And they were partially published long after the actual trial.

Then, Chris Ramsden and his team actually found the son of one of the original investigators, and they found microfilm tapes in his basement - which they then analyzed. They had a whole study that wasn't published!

So they found this hidden data that they were able to republish, regarding Minnesota Coronary and Sydney Diet Heart Trials. I think these two randomized controlled trials are important not to ignore.

Let's start with the Minnesota Coronary: Again, you can see Chris Ramsden is the first author and this one was published in 2016.

> *Re-evaluation of the traditional diet-heart hypothesis: Analysis of recovered data from Minnesota Coronary Experiment (1968-73). (11)*

Neither of these 2009 articles that are cited in this expert review [by Mazafarian] which was just quoted by the fact checkers, accounted for the fact that there's a 2016 paper and another 2018 paper from Chris Ramsden looking at the re-analysis of Minnesota Coronary and Sydney Diet Heart.

In short, this was a five-year trial with over 9,000 patients. And it showed that when you give people more linoleic acid rich vegetable oil, their cholesterol does go down. **But:**

> *There was a 22% higher risk of death for each 30 milligrams per deciliter reduction in serum cholesterol in the covariate adjusted Cox regression models.*

Oh, that's not very convenient, is it? How do we hide that? Well, we just exclude that study for some reason from Mazafarian's 2009 meta-analysis of the RCTS.

If you look in this paper, you can see the Kaplan-Meyer curves looking at the survival of people: Especially those above 65 fare very poorly - and the women look like they're faring even more poorly than the men, in terms of increased rates of death as their cholesterol is decreased.

Now interestingly, in this paper Chris Ramsden has done a great thing. He did a revised forest plot of the trials looking at seed oils.

Actually, according to this re-analysis, the overall hazard ratio looks like seed oils are quite harmful. So if we look at the best randomized control trials we have for seed oils, they don't look very good!

Now, there are methodological problems with perhaps every single one of these trials. And any time that I get into a disagreement with someone online about seed oils, we will go back and forth about whether the Minnesota Coronary or the Sidney Diet Heart study was reasonably conducted.

What I do know is that the LA Veterans Administration trial had significantly more smokers in the control group, which had less seed oils and *more saturated fat.* So that's going to confound things because smokers are more likely to have negative cardiovascular events. There are other trials, the Oslo Diet Heart trial had similar problems.

If you do the research and you really look at these trials:

- The Oslo Diet Heart
- The Finnish Health Study
- The LA Veterans Study,

all of the studies that show that seed oils are beneficial for humans had some pretty serious methodological flaws!

Now, to be fair: Critics of what I'm saying will point out that Minnesota Coronary had methodological flaws. To which I would say

„Yes, the patients in Minnesota Coronary - over 9,000 of them did go in and out of the hospital. But there were still a significant number of patients who were in the hospital for a sustained amount of time."

People will also look at Minnesota Coronary and Sidney Diet Heart and say „The margarine used had trans fats," suggesting that the seed oil group was getting more margarine / had more trans fats, and that's why I looked bad.

Well, this doesn't really hold up to careful consideration. Because what Ansel Keys knew, and what we know very clearly, is that:

When you have trans fats, your LDL goes up. But as you see from the Minnesota Coronary study results, the LDL goes down in the people who are getting the vegetable oil group.

So how could there be a significant amount of trans fats in their food, enough to make it invalid, enough to make their increased rates of death invalid, relative to the saturated fat group? Who was almost certainly eating the same trans fat laden margarine in the trial. How is there enough there, if their LDL went down? So there's a lot of problems.

Again, we get into a kind of like a high school cafeteria food fight about all of this. But it's important to point out that when we're looking at the RCTs, there's a lot of disagreement about this.

This is why respectful open discourse is so important. And this is why the AFP simply tagging my posts with partial misinformation and them just quoting Dariush Mozaffarian, saying „Hey, seed oils are helpful, they're not harmful" is very dangerous. Because it quells most of the discussions which could help a lot of people.

I'll also show the Sidney Diet Heart study re-analysis right here. Again, Chris Ramsden. This one was republished in 2013:

> *Use of dietary linoleic acid for secondary prevention of coronary heart disease and death: evaluation of recovered data from the Sydney Diet Heart Study and updated metaanalysis. (12)*

You can see here in the results:

> *The intervention group [the ones eating more omega-6 fats] had higher rates of death than controls, higher rates of cardiovascular disease than controls and higher rates of coronary heart disease than controls.*
> *Inclusion of these recovered data in an updated meta-analysis of linoleic acid intervention trials showed non-significant trends toward increased risks of death from coronary heart disease and cardiovascular disease.*

Which would make sense, when you consider the randomized controlled trials that I showed you before. Suggesting that oxidized LDL goes up, LP(a) goes up, CEPI-CT gets worse - which is the endothelial marker of vascular function.

What we have here is a pretty significant set of data which needs to be looked at very clearly. I think that for AFP factcheck to say that *claims that seed oils are harmful* are unsupported is patently false!

They only looked at Darius Mazafarian's opinion. As we've seen in his 2009 meta-analysis, he excluded many important trials, like Sydney Diet Heart, Minnesota Coronary trial and others. And he conflated omega-3s with omega-6s etc.

So there's a lot of discussion here that is much more nuanced than that simple AFP factchecker article would like you to know. There are a few more claims that I talked about in that reel that I want to show you.

If you have questions about the amount of canola oil trans fats, you can read this study:

> *A rapid method for the quantification of fatty acids in fats and oils with emphasis on trans fatty acids using Fourier transform near infrared spectroscopy. (13)*

This study has been cited by many on both sides of the aisle, regarding seed oils: Again, that canola oils generally have 1.9 to 3.6% trans fatty acids. These trans fatty acid, remember, are different than the trans fatty acids found in animal foods.

There is a often quoted blog post from a Harvard doctor, saying that animal foods have the same amount of trans fats, so why would you worry about the trans fat in canola oil?

Well, the ones from animal fats have been associated with beneficial outcomes, whereas the plant ones have clearly been associated with harmful outcomes. I don't even think people who believe that seed oils are benign or even helpful for humans would debate that point.

For the sake of completeness, I will show the 2009 paper in Circulation of which Dariush Mozaffarian is an author:

Omega-6 fatty acids and risk of cardiovascular disease.(14)

On a positive note, this paper is looking at only omega-6s and cardiovascular disease.

On a negative note, if you look at this paper, it is fraught with mistruths, misinformation and misconceptions about the studies I mentioned.

This one is from 2009, so it does not take into account the 2013 and 2016 reanalysis of Chris Ramsden's work, looking at the Sidney Diet Heart and Minnesota Coronary trials. And I think those are the best randomized controlled trials we have.

You can look at all of this and make your own judgments. This is all about thing thinking for yourself and not muzzling any side of the issue.

I would never want anyone claiming that *seed oils are beneficial for humans* to have a misinformation tag on their label. What I would want is for there to be respectful healthy discourse, that is done in a way that the lay public can understand. So that people can learn and understand that there is a lot of nuance in these studies.

There is certainly evidence that seed oils are very harmful for humans! This is something we have never eaten evolutionarily!

And this podcast is just the tip of the iceberg. Please refer back to the podcast I did with Jeff Nobbs from Zero Acre and Tucker Goodrich, in which we went into much more detail about seed oils and omega-6 fats.

We talked about anthropology, the fact that there are groups in all over the world who are very healthy - until they see seed oils! That doesn't really stand up to published randomized controlled trial evidence, but I think these anthropology natural experiments are also not to be ignored.

Hunter-gatherers only really have 2 to 3% of their calories in linoleic acid! We've never done this, this is a horrible human experiment. And I have fear, that seed oils are the single greatest driver of chronic disease in humans!

Maybe I'm right. Maybe I'm wrong. But we need to be able to have that conversation.

I will share yet another paper from Chris Ramsden:

> *Lowering dietary linoleic acid reduces bioactive oxidized linoleic acid metabolites in humans.(15)*

Clearly, OXLAMs (oxidative products of linoleic acid metabolism) like 4-HNE are reduced when you eat less linoleic acid. Things I've talked about with Tucker and Jeff Nobbs.

Just in case that wasn't enough to convince you: Consider this trial, the title says it all:

> *Dietary olive oil reduces low-density lipoprotein uptake by macrophages and decreases the susceptibility of the lipoprotein to undergo lipid peroxidation.(16)*

Tell me again that seed oils are not harmful for humans and are not linked to cardiovascular disease!

In summary I did a post on Instagram. In which I talked about

- The harms of canola oil
- The trans fats in canola oil

The fact that canola oil is from a rapeseed plant which has been genetically bred to be lower erucic acid. Erucic acid is a harmful thing!

And I talked about the fact that in the processing, canola oil is subjected to heat and oxidation, leading to trans fatty acids.

There's hexane in the canola oil

Seed oils - like canola oil - look very bad in randomized controlled trials for many health outcomes. Cardiovascular disease being one.

Interestingly, another video I did talking about seed oils as a driver of macular degeneration based on multiple observational studies was flagged and taken down on TikTok. I got a strike, saying that seed oils were linked to blindness in the United States and in the world.

Well, macular degeneration happens to be the number one cause of blindness in the world! So we could make a reasonable argument that seed oils could be the main driver of blindness.

But that post was taken down from TikTok! So we are in an environment, where bucking the norm or talking about things that are outside of the mainstream is not tolerated and that is very dangerous.

I'm not saying I have all the answers. I'm not saying I know everything about seed oils or LDL or lipoproteins or cardiovascular disease.

What I am saying is that I hope all of us can stand up for and urge anyone in control of such things, to allow us to live in a world where open free respectful discourse is king. And we can have differing opinions and we can discuss them so that everyone can learn. (...)

Hopefully, this has been helpful - and I hope you guys are doing well!

References

1)Factchecker article: https://factcheck.afp.com/doc.afp.com.333B473
2) Dayton S et al:
Composition of lipids in human serum and adipose tissue during prolonged feeding of a diet high in unsaturated fat.
J Lipid Res 1966; Jan; 103-11
3) Reaven P et al:
Effects of oleate-rich and linoleate-rich diets on the susceptibility of low density lipoprotein to oxidative modification in mildly hypercholesterolemic subjects. J Clin Invest 1993; Feb; 668-76
4) Jenkinson A et al:
Dietary intakes of polyunsaturated fatty acids and indices of oxidative stress in human volunteers.
Eur J Clin Nutr. 1999; Jul; 523-8
5) Kim M et al:
Impact of 8-week linoleic acid intake in soy oil on Lp-PLA2 activity in healthy adults.
Nutr Metab (Lond) 2017; May; 14:32
6) Berry EM et al:
Effects of diets rich in monounsaturated fatty acids on plasma lipoproteins--the Jerusalem Nutrition Study: high MUFAs vs high PUFAs.
Am J Clin Nutr. 1991; Apr; 899-907

7) Goldstein JL et al:
Binding site on macrophages that mediates uptake and degradation of acetylated low density lipoprotein, producing massive cholesterol deposition.
Proc Natl Acad Sci USA 1979; Jan; 333-7

8)Meisinger C et al:
Plasma oxidized low-density lipoprotein, a strong predictor for acute coronary heart disease events in apparently healthy, middle-aged men from the general population.
Circulation 2005; Aug; 651-7

9)Willeit P et al:
Low-Density Lipoprotein Cholesterol Corrected for Lipoprotein(a) Cholesterol, Risk Thresholds, and Cardiovascular Events.
J Am Heart Assoc. 2020; Dec; e016318

10) Mozaffarian D et al:
Effects on coronary heart disease of increasing polyunsaturated fat in place of saturated fat: a systematic review and meta-analysis of randomized controlled trials. PLoS Med. 2010; Mar; e1000252

11) Ramsden CE et al:
Re-evaluation of the traditional diet-heart hypothesis: analysis of recovered data from Minnesota Coronary Experiment (1968-73).
BMJ 2016; Apr; 353:i246

12) Ramsden CE et al:
Use of dietary linoleic acid for secondary prevention of coronary heart disease and death: evaluation of recovered data from the Sydney Diet Heart Study and updated meta-analysis.
BMJ 2013; Feb; 346:e8707

13) Azizian H, Kramer JKG:
A rapid method for the quantification of fatty acids in fats and oils with emphasis on trans fatty acids using Fourier Transform near infrared spectroscopy (FT-NIR). Lipids 2005; Aug; 855-67

14) Harris WS, Mozaffarian D et al:
Omega-6 Fatty Acids and Risk for Cardiovascular Disease.
Circulation 2009; 119:902-907

15) Ramsden CE et al:
Lowering dietary linoleic acid reduces bioactive oxidized linoleic acid metabolites in humans.
Prostaglandins Leukot Essent Fatty Acids. 2012; Oct-Nov 135-41

16) Aviram M, Eias K et al:
Dietary olive oil reduces low-density lipoprotein uptake by macrophages and decreases the susceptibility of the lipoprotein to undergo lipid peroxidation.
Ann Nutr Metab. 1993; 37(2):75-84

Chapter 2
How seed oils make you fat.
With Tucker Goodrich and Jeff Nobbs.

Dr. Paul Saladino:
All right! Tucker, Jeff welcome to the podcast! Thanks for being here, guys.

Tucker Goodrich:
Thanks for having us!

Jeff Nobbs:
Yeah thanks, Paul!

Dr. Saladino:
I'm super excited to have this conversation about seed oils with you guys. Tucker, you've been on the podcast at least once or twice before.

Jeff, this is your first time on the podcast. But you were gracious enough to let me use many of the graphics that came from your excellent blogs in my *Carnivore Code Cookbook*, and I threw them up on the screen during the Joe Rogan podcast. So thanks for all of that.

For people that don't know you: What are you up to now? And then we'll get into all of this. Tucker, what are you doing?

Goodrich:
I am spending a huge percentage of my time working with Jeff's team on getting the research message out there about the health problems with seed oils. As well as doing some podcasting and keeping up with spreading the message on Twitter and stuff like that.

When you asked me to do this, one of the reasons I suggested that Jeff should be part of this is that Jeff was a huge influence on the final version of the Zero Acres obesity post. And unlike a lot of CEOs, he's actually invested in this product. Meaning he's a real believer, he's not just a business guy.

Jeff had a lot of impact on this. He knows the science and he had a huge impact on how this final post came out, and what was included in the messages that were in it.

Dr. Saladino:
Yeah, that that blog post at Zero Acre was one of the reasons I thought we should do another podcast, because it's very excellent.

There's also a white paper on seed oils and cardiovascular disease there. These are very well referenced, very well written white papers. I really appreciate what you guys are doing there.

So Jeff: What is Zero Acre and what have you created there?

Nobbs:

Zero Acre is where I'm spending most of my time. This project is one of the solutions to the problem of seed oils at scale. It's why we started Zero Acre. We're making alternatives to seed oils, made by fermentation. Our first product is called *Cultured Oil*.

And I've been banging my head against the wall for the better part of the last decade on how we get seed oils out of the food system.

My background is in food, I have some restaurants and work with other food brands. And seed oils are just in everything! I'm preaching to the choir here... you guys know this.

At Zero Acre, we're trying to not only make products that can replace seed oils, but also educate on the issues with seed oils.

That's what we did with the white papers that we talked about.

Dr. Saladino:

Awesome, yeah! When I was recently in Phoenix, I did this bit of content where I went to a number of semi-fast food restaurants.

I went to Chipotle, I went to a Mongolian Grill, I went to a restaurant - and I asked them what cooking oils they use. Under the guise of saying „Oh, I have an allergy to these oils!" Because we could say that most humans probably have an ‚allergy' to seed oils in some way, shape or form.

But, I asked them what oils *do you use...* and they all uses seed oils, invariably! The only place that did not use seed oils was Smash Burger. We found out later they actually *do* use canola oil, but didn't tell me they used canola oil!

The Mongolian grill said they cover the grill in canola oil. They soak it in canola oil at night. They said „You can't ever eat here if you have an allergy because our food is literally drenched in canola oil."

All the other Yogi grills and stuff would either use soybean oil or canola oil. They use it in their fryers, they use it on their grill tops.

The restaurants would say they use olive oil and canola oil. When you actually look at the olive oil, it's usually not good quality. It's not extra virgin olive oil, it's not like a cold pressed olive oil. 34

Went to a Greek place, they had the cheapest, worst olive oil you can get - but they say olive oil. I went to Chipotle and they said it's rice bran oil which is actually pretty high in linoleic acid. And then they kicked us out „You can't film here, you can't film here!"

This is just to say that the mission you guys are a part of is really really important. I appreciate what you're doing, what Zero Acre is doing with the education and the cultured oil in general. Because these seed oils are ubiquitous...

Jeff, why don't you just start us off?

Goodrich:

Just one point there: Education is awesome and lots of people have responded to this and said „Well, I'll just stop eating it." And yes, that's great. That's a great alternative for an individual, just to change their diet.

But when 20% of our food supply in the United States is seed oils at this point, you can't just cut that out of the food supply. Right?

You need an alternative.

Dr. Saladino:

Yes, that's a very good point, you can't just cut it out of the food supply.

I know our mutual friend Anthony Gustin has thought about this as well. Unfortunately, there's probably not enough cows to make butter and tallow to replace all of the seed oil in the world. So we need something elso to do that. That's definitely a valuable thing that Zero Acre is doing.

So Jeff: What are seed oils - at a high level? Why do we think that they're potentially bad for us?

Nobbs:

Oh man! We don't want this podcast to be 6 hours, right?

Dr. Saladino:

No we don't, haha!

Nobbs:

I'll give the abridged version... so what are seed oils? Seed oils compared to vegetable oils, those terms are kind of used interchangeably. But technically, vegetable oils are the broader category of any oil that comes from a plant or a crop.

Whether that's
- Olive
- Palm
- Avocado
- Coconut

Or
- Corn
- Canola
- Soybean
- Sunflower

Seed oils are a subcategory of vegetable oils that include oils that come specifically from seeds or grains. Which are technically the seeds of grasses.

So sunflower seed oil, rape seed oil (also known as canola oil), soybean oil, rice bran oil... that's what seed oils are.

We've talked about **linoleic acid** and omega-6 fats a lot. And the reason that those terms are somewhat synonymous with seed oils is because seed oils have by far the highest content of these fats.

These fats are found in all foods, in very low amounts. But in seed oils they're found in abundance, orders of magnitude more than in any other food.

Throughout this conversation, we'll be talking about linoleic acid and omega-6, as well as seed oils. And I think we can use those terms interchangeably for that reason.

Dr. Saladino:
And at a high level: Why do we think they're bad for us?

Nobbs:
I think it starts with evolutionary precedence.

Nutrition is probably the worst form of science, in that most of our nutrition science today is driven more by politics than actual science! There's actually very little that's scientific about how we currently make nutrition decisions.

So it's helpful to have other frameworks that we can look at, to figure out what should we be eating. And evolutionary biology and our evolutionary precedent is an important one.

Looking at the diets of human populations that aren't sick and aren't obese, and looking at what they eat and what they don't eat. Those are really valuable frameworks, at least as a starting point.

So why are they bad for us? First and foremost, there's no history of humans eating them. And usually, when we introduce new molecules and compounds into our diets in unprecedented amounts, it doesn't end well for us.

I think linoleic acid and seed oils are no exception. So purely from a precedent standpoint, we haven't eaten them. And

- Any human population that starts eating seed oils inevitably becomes sick and obese. Similarly,
- There's no human population that is sick or obese, that doesn't consume seed oils in meaningful quantities

So that at the very least should throw up the red flag, that there's something worth looking into here.

I will say there are some studies that show some individuals are and stay healthy, eating seed oils. I liken it to smoking cigarettes and cancer:

There are plenty of individuals who smoke cigarettes and don't get lung cancer - but there's no population that picks up cigarette smoking in large amounts that doesn't also have increased rates of lung cancer.

So at a *population level*, something is going on here.

Then you take it to the next step of more *observational studies*: People who tend to have more dietary linoleic acid, what are their outcomes? They tend to be worse.

Take it a step further and look at *randomized controlled trials*: There are several randomized controlled trials showing far worse health outcomes. Whether it's obesity, heart disease or all cause mortality with an increased consumption of seed oils.

Kind of broadly, you go from population level data to observational studies to randomized controlled trials.

Then from there, there's also just common sense of: How much real food would you have to eat in order to actually get the amount of oil, that's in like a restaurant meal or a bag of chips.

Tucker could get into the mechanistic details and data of what happens when we actually eat seed oils. I mean, there's fascinating research, showing high linoleic acid seed oils... It's not just the linoleic acid, but what does that linoleic acid turn into? Either in the frying pan or in your body.

What that linoleic acid turns into is potentially far worse than the linoleic acid itself! These metabolic products are objectively, uncontroversially toxic. More so chronically than acutely, like ingesting arsenic - but still toxic!

Another important point regarding the science: We're typically using seed oils to cook our food.

But many of the studies that are done on seed oils are investigating them in a fresh state, uncooked. That's probably not appropriate, since we mostly eat cooked seed oils, and seed oils go from bad to far worse, the longer we cook them. There's all sorts of data showing that.

The last point - just because I think it's underappreciated - is how bad seed oils are for the environment!

There's so much talk of red meat being bad for the environment... Vegetable oils, broadly speaking, those plants take up more land than than any other crop.

They're about a third of global croplands! Leading to all sorts of issues with biodiversity loss and deforestation. This is pretty much uncontroversial, the data is very clear. We're destroying a big part of our planet to grow these crops, that end up ultimately doing us harm. Killing us.

Dr. Saladino:
Great introduction! So many rabbit holes to go down there...
Tucker, you want to add something?

Goodrich:
Yeah, very good points made by Jeff! I just would like to say that, as we start talking about the epidemiology, people often say to me „Well, the epidemiology doesn't support this." To emphasize the points that he was making:

When you start looking at this on a population level, there are no populations that avoid seed oils that have the health problems, with the chronic diseases, that those populations that have high levels do have!

I've looked, I've asked people, I've yet to find a single exception!

When you start getting into trying to figure out what an ubiquitous element in the food supply is doing, as most epidemiologists are doing... If you're looking at people in the United States, everybody in the United States has been consuming high amounts of seed oils for over 150 years.

And what the science clearly shows is that the negative effects of these seed oils seem to start at fairly low amounts. So if you're saying „Okay. Well, everybody in America roughly eats 7% seed oils and some people are doing okay."

You know, the number of people in the United States who are metabolically unhealthy, the highest number I've heard is 92 percent! So when those guys are doing epidemiology, they're looking at an almost entirely sick population. 38

And in my opinion, it's super difficult to take that fact, turn it around and say „Well, these aren't problematic! Because look, 8% of the people are healthy!"

Dr. Saladino:
Super important points! It's great that in the white paper on seed oils and obesity on the Zero Acre blog, you guys start with the discussion of this anthropology. You point out the Tsimané: Maybe you could tell us the story of the Bolivian Tsimané people and their exposure to seed oils...

I think this anthropology is a good framework for this discussion. And I love what you guys both pointed out, that indigenous huntergatherer type populations generally don't consume...

I shouldn't even say generally: They consistently and invariably do not consume more than 2 to 3% of their calories from seed oils.

Goodrich:
There is at least one exception of that. We'll get into that, because it's the exception that proves the rule, in my opinion.

Dr. Saladino:
Perfect! Yeah, you can tell us about that.

So, ancestral eating populations don't consume more than 3% - and the American population consumes 7 to 10% of their calories from seed oils.

Now, 2 to 3% versus 7 to 10% may not sound like it's a lot - but it's really important to understand that the actual negative health effects of those oils are probably already seen at a very low percentage level.

So going from 8 to 10% of linoleic acid in your diet may actually not have a measurable negative consequence! This is a very important point when it comes to understanding the nuance of the research.

Yeah, if you guys want to talk a little bit about these indigenous populations... what they're like in terms of health - and what happens when they're exposed to these oils. I think that's a good place to start, sort of anthropologically.

Nobbs:
I'll let Tucker speak. Just wanted to clarify ,Paul: The 7 to 10% number is linoleic acid in our diet. And it's more than twice that for general seed oil consumption. [In calories]

Dr. Saladino:
Perfect, thank you.

Goodrich:
So the Tsimané are a population living in the Amazonian rainforest in Bolivia. They are the favorite population at the moment of cardiologists. Because they went down there and discovered that they have essentially no heart disease. The lowest of any population ever explored.

And of course they also don't have the other things that tend to go along with that. They don't have obesity, low very rates of obesity. Then they don't have diabetes, they don't have any of these other problems.

These are poor people living in the jungle. They live by doing a lot of farming, they have a pretty high carbohydrate diet. In some of the interviews I've seen with them, they complain about how they can't get enough meat to eat, so they're always hungry. But by the standards of Americans, they are very healthy.

These folks and the Kitavaans (who are a South Pacific group) are two of the populations that have been eating what you could call *an ancestral diet.* They're not hunter-gatherers, they're not a model for the carnivore diet - these folks eat a lot of plant matter!

But what they haven't been eating - up until recently - are what the research studies called ‚market foods'. They get their own food out of the Amazonian jungle.

Then they noticed that things were starting to change. They initially noticed that there was a correlation between motorboat use and the beginnings of obesity in this population.

And you might think to yourself „Why on Earth would having a motorboat make you fat?" The answer turned out to be, if you have a motorboat you can get go down the river and get to a store and start buying market foods.

So the researchers turned around and they looked at what are these folks actually eating. And they found out that the correlation with obesity in this population is their increased intake of industrial vegetable oils, that they are getting from stores.

And like every other population on earth, the more exposed they get to an industrial diet, they start eating the same foods - which means refined carbohydrates, processed foods and seed oils.

So, these folks are in the process of leaving their ancestral way of living aside, going to a modern diet. And we're already starting to see the negative effects of that diet on this population.

What's likely going to follow are the same things that follow everywhere else. Which is heart disease... and in 20 years, we'll be reading papers about

„Paradox: The Tsimané eat an AHA approved prudent diet, yet they have high rates of heart disease! Versus when they were just living off the jungle, they were all healthy."

I mean, it's entertaining to see this happen, in kind of a sad way.

Dr. Saladino:

It's like the *Israeli Paradox:* That Israelis eat a heck of a lot of seed oils - I think some of the highest amounts in the world - and yet, they have the same or higher rates of heart disease, diabetes and obesity as other parts of the world.

I don't understand. All the paradoxes I've ever heard of, are not paradoxes! You know,

How can the Eskimos eat so much fat and not get heart disease? Well, because they're not eating processed foods. *How can the French...*

Like, none of these paradoxes - the Eskimo Paradox, the French Paradox - none of these seem like paradoxes from an ancestralevolutionary perspective.

But when viewed through the lens of what is widely considered to be a healthy diet, they're all paradoxical. I don't understand why people don't realize, like „Wait! Maybe the lens, maybe the whole overarching paradigm is wrong!"

Goodrich:

To Jeff's point about nutrition science: In real science, a paradox means *your hypothesis is probably wrong.* And you do occasionally get something like the Black Hole, which was initially thought to be a paradox in physics - and then they discovered they actually exist.

But the French Paradox or the Israeli Paradox are very easily explained: Our understanding of the effect of omega-6 polyunsaturated fats on the human body is simply wrong!

And thinking that we're going to eat more of them and get healthier... I mean, we've been going down that road for 150 years.

What I keep asking the advocates of consuming omega-6 polyunsaturated fats is: We've gone to the point where we're consuming an enormous amount of these - when do we start seeing the health benefits?

Do you have to get to 20%, and then all of a sudden you stop being obese, diabetic and dying of heart disease exactly? When's the tipping point?

Nobbs:

Yeah, we're still not eating enough! You see that in the U.S Dietary Guidelines...

We've seen this exponential rise in the consumption of seed oils.

You know, a 1000x increased since 1909 in soybean oil alone.

And the Dietary Guidelines say *we're still not eating enough!*

Basically, what a seed oil proponent would say to Tucker, it's that: „We still got to eat a little bit more" to get to the holy land of of perfect health. I mean, it's just a total bonkers response. Because we used to not eat any of this stuff, and we were in really great health.

Dr. Saladino:

If we eat more seed oils, our LDL could be even lower! And as we'll talk about later in the podcast, we would still have more oxidized LDL and LP(a), which everyone ignores.

But lowering your LDL with seed oils must be a good thing, guys. This paradigm must be true! We all know it's true!

Nobbs:

Look at the actual health outcomes or all cause mortality outcomes, let's just look at the biomarkers.

I wrote a whole post on the issues with observational studies because they're the backbone for how we make nutritional decisions in this country. They sound really big and important:

You see a 400,000 person study from Harvard researchers that spans 20 years - and most people would think „How can that be wrong?" or „How could that be more wrong than a 7-year trial with just a few hundred people?"

Not understanding the difference between a randomized controlled trial and an observational study.

Paul, you've talked about this in the past, the healthy user bias: As soon as we started recommending seed oils as a heart healthy alternative, anyone who cared about their health...

You know, they did yoga and lifted weights, ate more fruit and whatever - they then also added more seed oils. Because they were like „Oh, that's what healthy people do!"

So as soon as that happened, any observational data should have just been completely thrown out the window. **There's no amount of controlling you can do to account for healthy user bias.** But sadly, those kinds of studies still drive most of our nutrition policy.

Dr. Saladino:
Tucker, what is the exception to the rule, regarding the indigenous populations that you were mentioning earlier?

Goodrich:
It's the Bushmen in Africa, the !Kung.

They seasonally eat something called a mangongo nut. And the mangongo nut, like most seeds, has a high amount of linoleic acid in it. So seasonally, when they're eating these nuts, they get high amounts of linoleic acid. And what does that do to them?

Well, it makes them insulin resistant! They can't pass an oral glucose tolerance test when they are on the mangongo nut part of their diet.

So the only ancestral group we have, who does not eat a low seed oil diet, is also the only ancestral group we know of that can't pass an oral glucose tolerance test!

And that includes folks like the Eskimos, the Inuit - who've never seen a carbohydrate bigger than a blueberry – nevertheless, they are perfectly able to pass a glucose tolerance test normally. So we're left with this one little group, who eats lots of mangongo nuts seasonally because they have nothing better to eat They would prefer to eat meat, but they can't.

When you take them out of that environment, if they go into a reservation where they're no longer eating these mangongo nuts seasonally... then this diabetic effect of the nuts goes away.

Dr. Saladino:

It's pretty interesting, yeah. I've visited the Hadza in Tanzania and I'd want to visit the !Kung.

Richard Lee has done a lot of research, and in his book he talks about the fact that when they get meat, they eat it with quite enjoyment. And they can eat up to two kilograms of meat per day.

Similar to the Hadza. Basically, the amount of meat eaten in these hunter-gatherer cultures is proportional only to the availability of the meat. But there is a time of year when they eat these mangongo nuts.

If we had a time machine, we could solve so many problems in nutritional science. If we just had a time machine, I'd love to go back 30 to 50 000 years, and see how the ancestors of these huntergatherers ate.

Who we believe to be a good proxy for where we've come from as humans, to see how they were actually living. Also, to see whether they were eating that many mangongo nuts voluntarily or whether this mangongo nut preference is a result of infringement on their hunting lands or changes in the actual ecosystems in which they find themselves.

Because certainly with the Hadza, there is a lot of infringement on their hunting grounds and they cannot hunt the animals they want to hunt anymore. So they're forced to eat foods that are not necessarily ancestral.

They still want to do that, but they can't get as much as they would like. Kind of like the Tsimané.

Goodrich:

It's an important point to note that humans have probably been eating seeds and nuts for a very long time. I mean, they found evidence of grain consumption amongst the Neanderthals by looking at dental calculus - the plaque that your dentist takes off your teeth.

What's changed in our diet is using industrial processes to extract massive amounts of these fats out of seeds and nuts. Jeff put awesome date together of how much corn does it take to produce corn oil. And it's like an enormous amount!

I mean, if you eat corn on the cob, it's not really oily. It's not like an avocado or an olive. It takes industrial processing to get seed oil out of seeds, for the most part.

Dr. Saladino:

60 to 90 ears of corn for 5 tablespoons of oil, right Jeff?

40

Nobbs:
Yeah! I don't know about you, I have never been able to put down 60 ears of corn.

Dr. Saladino:
We did the calculations... I don't know if you shared this one as well, but we tried to recalculate 2.5 pounds of sunflower seeds if they're in the hull.

And I don't know what it is for soybeans, it's got to be on the order of 1 to 2 pounds of soybeans. You may know off the top of your head, Jeff.

Nobbs:
Multiple cups of soybeans, yeah.

Dr. Saladino:
...to get the equivalent of 5 to 7 tablespoons of seed oil, which is what the average American eats in a day.

Nobbs:
Yes. You'd have to have a really, really long baseball game in order to get through multiple pounds of sunflower seeds!

That points to... just because it's from a food that is a real whole food, does not mean by definition that it's good for you, or even okay for you.

You just wouldn't be able to eat that many sunflower seeds or that many ears of corn. Even if you somehow did, you probably wouldn't feel like eating it again for many months.

Yet, most Americans - and increasingly the rest of the world - are not only eating this amount on a daily basis, but on a per meal basis. That all averages out to eating that every single day, day in day out, for most people's lives. Sort of no wonder that leads to chronic disease.

It's not like you're going to keel over and die after that one meal, or after a week of eating that way. But you do that for months, years, decades – it will lead to all sorts of health issues.

Goodrich:
It gets back to the parallel of smoking: If you smoke a pack of cigarettes once, you're probably going to be nauseous, but you're not going to get lung cancer from it. You're not going to get all the other diseases that come from smoking.

I mean, even for lung cancer you need to smoke for 20 years or so. And smoking's about as noxious a thing as it's possible for a human to do.

Nobbs:
Paul, it's about 5 cups of cooked soybeans for 5 tablespoons of soybean oil.

Dr. Saladino:
Thank you. That's a lot of soybeans!

I think it also speaks to a really interesting idea, that perhaps our exposure to linoleic acid may have been seasonal in our history and that increased consumption of nuts and seeds may have happened in the winter or the fall.

And perhaps that did lead to some increase in obesity, which was beneficial for humans living hundreds of thousands of years ago - during an actual winter period, when food may have been more scarce. So perhaps there is a mechanism here.

We now essentially live in an eternal summer, in the fact that we don't have food scarcity. Most of us are quite fortunate to have access to foods all of the time. We go to the grocery store which are our modern day hunting grounds, and they're stocked the same every day.

But at the same time as we're living in an eternal summer in terms of food availability, it's almost like we're living in an eternal winter, in terms of the signals we're giving our bodies by eating this many seed oils every day.

I think that's an interesting parallel. It makes sense to me from an evolutionary context and is quite a compelling hypothesis.

Nobbs:
Yeah, and we talk about this at ZeroAcre.com/Obesity. There is the white paper that we're referencing where we go into detail on this.

I think it's fair to say that we don't know for sure why exactly increased consumption of seed oils lead to increased weight gain and obesity. Also we can't say for sure that they do, but that's the case of most things in nutrition.

Studies seem to point to certain outcomes. Or evolutionarily, certain things would happen when we ate different types of food. But there are a number of studies that show increased consumption of linoleic acid and seed oils do lead to weight gain.

So then the question is: Why does that happen?

Goodrich:
That's in animals and in humans.

Nobbs:
Yeah, exactly. And one explanation is what you're describing, Paul. That it could be an evolutionarily conserved mechanism, from small

rodents to other primates and potentially even humans, where it's like *Winter is coming, time to put on weight in a time of food scarcity.*

So around fall time, there are nuts and seeds that are available for consumption, maybe some grains. And we consume more of those and our bodies get the signal that it's time to put on weight. There are interesting examples in other mammals and in other animals, where they're actually unable to put on weight and enter hibernation - unless they consume more linoleic acid!

So if you take that to the practical extreme, like you said:

- *Humans are in a constant state of hibernation and weight gain because we're constantly preparing for winter.*

And if other animals are any indication, without that increased amount of linoleic acid, we're not in a state of hibernation. Meaning more energy, being more aware, less weight gain. That's one hypothesis that we talked about in the white paper.

Another one is that there's no intentionality. It's simply:

- *Something's gone wrong, something breaks and that leads to increased fat storage.*

That gets into what linoleic acid turns into in our body, and how that toxins start breaking things, leading to fat gain. That hypothesis is less about an evolutionarily conserved intentional mechanism and more about things just going wrong.

Goodrich:

Even that effect that you're just describing is evolutionarily conserved. They've shown it in bacteria and roundworms, all the way up to humans. So it seems to be...

I mean, what we're talking about here really are fundamental processes that we've kicked sideways by overconsumption of these fats.

Even some of the toxins that we're discussing, HNE (which is probably the best studied oxidative product of linoleic acid) has signaling rules in the body. It's a fundamental part of our metabolism.

But it's supposed to be there in a certain quantity! And by dumping excess linoleic acid into our bodies in massive amounts, we seem to have increased the amount of this toxin.

And everywhere you look through chronic disease, in every single chronic disease, this toxin is thought to play a role! (...)

Dr. Saladino:

Let's get into HNE in one moment. I just want to share this great video of how canola oil is made. I think it speaks to a lot of the insanity, regarding this oil specifically.

Canola oil coming from a rape seed. Something that's never been a food for humans. It had to be I guess genetically modified, to lower the amount of erucic acid. You and I talked about this on the first podcast, Tucker.

CANOLA actually means *Canadian Oil Low Acid* - and that acid that's supposed to be low is the erucic acid. Which appears to have pretty negative effects in the heart. And yet, this is a massively common oil that comes from a seed that's never even really been a part of the human diet at all.

This is the Clip: *How it's made – Canola oil. [Dr. Saladino starts at 1:42 minutes]*

https://www.youtube.com/watch?v=gfrhcsWfG3g

47

[Female voice narrating over factory processing of yellow oil oil/sludge]

> *... it has a large revolving screw-shaped shaft enclosed within a slotted cage. As the shaft turns, its threads squeeze the flakes with high pressure, forcing out the oil which then drains out through the slots.*

> *42 % of canola seed is oil. This screw press extracts nearly three-quarters of that. The remainder is still trapped in the pressed flakes, now referred to as* canola cake. *This chemical extraction process removes all but a trace of oil.*

This is the hexane extration.

Nobbs:

My favorite part was the canola cake! I wonder how long it's going to be until that's being served at various bakeries.

Dr. Saladino:

Yes, that's totally true! So there was the hexane extraction, let's keep going: *[2:27]*

> *The factory then grinds the cake into protein-rich meal,* **which it sells as animal feed.** *The extracted oil, stored in large tanks, now enters the refinery phase.*

*First, they wash the oil for 20 minutes with sodium hydroxide. During this wash cycle, they spin the oil at high speed so that the centrifugal force separates the natural impurities, **which the factory later sells to soap manufacturers.***

After this cleaning process, the oil is visibly clearer. However, it still contains natural waxes which make it look cloudy. So the next step is to cool the oil to 5 degrees celsius. This thickens those waxes, so they can filter it.

*The waxes don't go to waste either: The factory uses them **to produce vegetable shortening.***

So this is what's in canola oil before it's refined. I just wanted to emphasize to people that these oils, whether it's corn, canola, safflower, sunflower, soybean, are
- refined
- bleached and
- deodorized oils.

Meaning they have to go through this heavy refining process. It may not look exactly like that for all of those oils. But in general, there's a
- grinding phase
- heating phase
- bleaching phase
- deodorizing phase. And a
- removal of the waxes phase.

This is what we're putting in our bodies! This is what some people in the nutrition space believe should be a part of our diets. **Goodrich:**

Paul, it makes my mouth water... I wish we hadn't scheduled this before lunch!

Dr. Saladino:

Canola cake for lunch! And we can drip some of the wax on top for you, Tucker! It's used to make vegetable shortening... the canola wax just on top of your canola cake. There you go, that's the diet of champions!

Goodrich:

After watching that:

One of the studies that we discuss in our obesity post, is one that Kevin Hall did. Which has gotten a lot of traction. Because he compared an ultra-processed diet to a non-processed diet. And one of the variables that he wasn't able to control for was the omega-6 content.

If you look at his results from an omega-6 causing obesity perspective, it's entirely consistent with that. Unfortunately, the definition of processed foods that they're using does *not* say that canola oil is a highly processed food - which is absurd!

I mean, you look at that making-of video and you say „That's totall equivalent to butter!" My grandmother could have made butter, it's easy to make butter. All you need is a little wooden drum and you spin some milk around and you've got butter.

It's impossible to make these seed oils in any quantity, using anything that anyone of our ancestors would have recognized. It's just impossible - and that's why we weren't eating them.

Dr. Saladino:

Yeah, we didn't have machines like that. A sodium hydroxide wash, a hexane extraction of the oil. It's crazy, we would never have gotten this amount of these oils in our diet.

Regarding the actual study from Kevin Hall, I've done some content on Instagram about the study:

> *Ultra-Processed Diets Cause Excess Calorie Intake and Weight Gain: An Inpatient Randomized Controlled Trial of Ad Libitum Food Intake*

Super fascinating! The ultra-processed diet group gains two pounds in two weeks - and the unprocessed diet group loses two pounds in two weeks! They're served the same amount of food, but they're ad-libitum, so they can eat as much as they want in the study.

The diets were matched for presented calories, fat, carbohydrates, protein, sodium and fiber. So they were trying to make it as consistent as possible.

And what you saw over and over was that in the ultra-processed diet, people ate more. They were more hungry, which led to more weight gain.

Even though they were trying to match for everything, they could not match for omega-6, presumably. As you're suggesting Tucker, the omega-6 content of the ultra-processed diet was higher.

This is foreshadowing things I want to talk about later, with these oils and hunger satiety signals.

Let's actually let's get into HNE: What it is, where it comes from and why it's so important? And what kind of research we have on HNE and its issues for humans.

Nobbs:

I'd just want to add that the refining of vegetable oils, seed oils, is particularly problematic because of the types of fats they contain, and what happens to them when they are processed like this.

The fact that we couldn't eat these oils before modern industrial processing just shows how near impossible it would have been to consume high amounts of linoleic acid.

There are plenty of studies showing that things like canola oil, when they go through this high heat processing:

Before they even go in the bottle, a lot of those polyunsaturated fats actually turn into trans fats! You know, everyone can at least agree we shouldn't be consuming massive amounts of trans fats! We tried that experiment, it didn't end well.

If you refine something like beef tallow, simply the process of refining doesn't immediately make it horrible for you. But the refining and high-heat processing of unstable fats makes them far worse!

Dr. Saladino:

And you have a blog post on the Zero Acre website about canola oil which is excellent! It points out the fact that according to the FDA or the USDA guidelines, if something contains less than 0.5 grams of trans fat **per serving**, you can say *it has no trans fat.*

But there are at least two studies, showing that when they actually look at the amount of these trans fats in oils (including canola oil), we find anywhere from 3.6 to 4.2% percent of the fats in canola oil are trans fats!

But when you do the math with the labeling, they're supposed to be less than 0.5 or 0.6% of these oils

Goodrich:

In a *food*, you're allowed to say *if it's less than half a percent,* that *there are no trans fats in the food.*

And if you're using canola as an *ingredient [of that food]*, then yes: By law, the manufacturer is allowed to misrepresent what's in the food. Thank you, FDA!

Dr. Saladino:

And in the white paper on cardiovascular disease and seed oils, you pointed out something that I wasn't aware of... we can go down this rabbit hole as well if you'd want.

You point out that there's research involving these trans fats and arterial damage. I've always wondered „What's so bad about trans fats?"

The point that I want to make here is that these seed oils contain more trans fats than people are being told - and there's good evidence these trans fats are damaging our arteries.

I don't think anyone in the nutrition community is defending trans fats now. We know these are harmful! And in these seed oils, they're present in way higher amounts than we're being told.

Goodrich:

Well, I'll defend them, just because I like to be a contrarian. I just want to make a distinction that the Dietary Guidelines fails to make: There are natural trans fats, found in dairy. The harmful ones are the synthetic trans fats.

The Dietary Guidelines don't make that distinction! They say „Oh, dairy contains trans fats, so therefore you shouldn't eat dairy!" That is a misrepresentation of the science.

Natural trans fats have been shown to be very beneficial, they're actually investigating them for anti-cancer treatments and protection against atherosclerosis. So there's a big difference there.

The synthetic trans fats that are produced exclusively from seed oils, from the partial hydrogenation of seed oils, are the ones that we need to be avoiding.

And yeah, your body never evolved to process these things: **They break your mitochondria** because it's a totally novel fat. As Jeff said, these new things tend to be problematic.

Dr. Saladino:

Yes, exactly. At the risk of confusing people, I'll try and preemptively answer a question. People will often ask me *what about conjugated linoleic acid?* Which is a trans fat found in dairy fat.

This is a different molecule! Conjugated linoleic acid is a different looking molecule at the fatty acid level than linoleic acid. It's similar in some ways, in terms of the number of carbons - but they look totally differently.

Goodrich:

Yeah, the formula is the same, it's just that the structure is a bit different. It is, as you said, part of dairy. And conjugated linoleic acid specifically, CLA, is the one that has been investigated for its health benefits, its anti-cancer benefits.

And amusingly, at least in breast cancer models and in animals, they think that it may be beneficial because it's blocking linoleic acid! Your body is taking CLA up instead of linoleic acid, and it doesn't have the negative effects of linoleic acid.

Except in large quantities, like all the rest of this stuff. So the amount you get in beef or dairy, great! But don't try superdosing CLA, that's probably not going to turn out well.

Dr. Saladino:

Doing things that are evolutionarily inconsistent is probably not a good idea for humans.

Nobbs:

Just when we thought nutrition couldn't get more confusing:

- Okay, Linoleic acid – Bad.
- Trans fats – Bad. But the
- Trans fat version of linoleic acid - Good!

[Everybody laughing]

Dr. Saladino:

Because it's evolutionarily consistent and it's something we would have been exposed to only in very small amounts! Let's also note that the amount of conjugated linoleic acid that people are getting in dairy fat is very small.

If we're talking absolute amounts, we're not talking anything like the amount of linoleic acid people would be getting in seed oils, when we're talking about conjugated linoleic acid from dairy and animal fat.

Goodrich:

Linoleic acid in those same quantities as CLA would probably be totally harmless. Because that's what we would have evolved to eat.

Dr. Saladino:

That's probably the amount of linoleic acid that all three of us are getting on a daily basis, because there is a small amount of linoleic acid in egg yolks, in the fat of my steak, in the hamburgers that I'm eating, in dairy. But it's a much smaller amount of linoleic acid.

I think tallow has about 2% linoleic acid... or butter is also around 2% linoleic acid. Relative to corn or let's say soybean oil, where it's 40 to 60% linoleic acid in those oils.

Goodrich:

That's a really important point. Because people hear that those things are bad and they're like „Oh well, then zero must be best!" - and that's not necessarily the case. If you're eating evolutionarily appropriate levels of probably any fat, you're gonna do just fine. As that's what the system was designed to handle.

Dr. Saladino:

Tucker, do you want to bring us down the HNE rabbit hole? I think this is a really important one for people to understand.

Goodrich:

Right! So HNE stands for 4-Hydroxynonenal. When you oxidize a linoleic acid molecule, it breaks in half - and HNE is one half of it.

Now, HNE is a great marker of the negative health effects of linoleic acid because it's only produced from linoleic acid. There are other markers that scientists use that can be produced from omega-6 or omega-3 fats. You know, different types of markers.

This one is specific to linoleic acid. And in the context of obesity, very interesting:

When they first discovered and started exploring HNE (which was discovered in the context of cancer research), they started adding it into cells in vitro. Treating cell cultures, basically. I think it was yeast... and they discovered that the yeast cells either died or got fat!

Which sort of establishes one of the important things about HNE: That it's toxic, it's a toxin! I mean, that's not my opinion, that's how it's listed everywhere you'll ever read it. In large amounts, this is a toxin.

It also alters how your body, your cell, processes energy, and it predisposes you to storing fat. So a continuous supply of HNE which you would only get in a lab - or if you're eating the modern American diet - is going to predispose your body to constantly storing fat.

They've discovered in these animal models that when you stop the flow of HNE, this process stops! But unfortunately, in the context of the modern American diet, you can't stop it because you're constantly eating it. 54

Every meal, you're exposed to these fats and they're breaking down into these toxins in your body. Probably that's the reason why one of the more interesting epidemiological studies that I've ever read found, that the most fattening food that Americans eat is french fried potatoes. By a huge margin, by 6 or 7 fold!

And one of the things that happens to the vegetable oils when you fry anything in it, particularly potatoes, is that it breaks down into this obesogenic toxin HNE.

Dr. Saladino:

The amount of HNE in french fries is pretty enormous, isn't it? You actually referenced the study in the blog post and I was looking for the study... because there's actually studies on HNE in french fries, right?

Goodrich:

In french fries, in any fried food where you're frying linoleic acid, it's going to break down into HNE and other toxins.

Some of them are obesogenic, some of them are thought to be carcinogenic. I mean, HNE... when they were trying to figure out exactly why LDL causes atherogenesis, the answer that they came to was HNE!

Because of the damaging, of the toxic effects that it has in the body.

Dr. Saladino:

Okay, let's advance to linking LDL and HNE. I want to highlight a few things that you said, that *the source for HNE in the human body is linoleic acid.* That's where it comes from, it's not coming from anywhere else.

Goodrich:

The only other place is from other omega-6 fats. So it can also be made from arachidonic acid, of which you typically only have a tiny amount in the body.

Dr. Saladino:

And perhaps we should have mentioned this earlier: The human body stores polyunsaturated fatty acids of your diet. So like chickens and pigs, like animals that are monogastric animals, we don't have a method to get rid of polyunsaturated fatty acids.

They end up in our adipose tissue, in some proportional amount to our consumption.

Goodrich:

If we're consuming them vastly in excess. We actually do have mechanisms to get rid of them. And it's thought that the harmful effects are the reason why our body treats it the way it does.

For instance, if you drink alcohol: Alcohol is a toxin, so your body preferentially starts burning the alcohol to get rid of it.

You do the same thing with glucose and you do the same thing with polyunsaturated fatty acids.

In fact, one of the things that your body does with polyunsaturated fats is it turns them into neutral, inert things like cholesterol or saturated fats.

The human body is a survival machine! We've been around for many millions of years, we got here because our bodies are good at processing this stuff and protecting us from harm.

And if you eat PUFAs, polyunsaturated fats, one of the things your body does is convert them into harmless things like cholesterol and saturated fat. That don't oxidize and don't become toxic.

Dr. Saladino:

But the outlet to the „toxic bathtub" is is not terribly large: The amount of polyunsaturated fatty acids flowing out, being converted, is just too small. In that way, these conversion capabilities are the bottleneck.

I've only seen like one kinetic study on how quickly we turn over polyunsaturated fats, let's just say omega-6 fats for this purposes of this discussion. It was something like 680 days is the half-life of those fatty acids in our tissues, or something similar astronomical.

So who knows how long it takes for these things to get out of our bodies, towards an ancestrally appropriate level. We can get rid of them, it's just a very slow process. Am I understanding that correctly?

Goodrich:

Yeah, that's right. And there are certainly things you can try to *accelerate the process.*

I mean, you've done lots of posts on the benefits of

- **Exercise** and
- **Fasting.** But the best thing to do is
- **Avoid them** in the first place

Dr. Saladino:

Let's talk about beta oxidation and ketogenic / low carb diets! Because I learned reading the white paper that one of the ways - or perhaps the main pathway - by which HNE is disposed of in the body, is beta oxidation. Which is part of the process of ketosis.

Goodrich:

Only in a ketogenic state is HNE oxidized.

Dr. Saladino:

Interesting!

Goodrich:

Yes! And I suspect that that is one of the benefits of the ketogenic diet: That it is allowing you to burn these toxins off as energy, rather than having them go out and do damage throughout your body.

Dr. Saladino:

That's really very interesting.

Goodrich:

Yeah! They've shown this in animal studies quite clearly. If you look at fat consumption of an American diet, using the quantities and the types of fats that we're consuming, in these studies:

At the low end, they're not very obesogenic. In the middle, they're very obesogenic. But then, when you get up to the high end, the curve starts to come back down again.

Part of the reason that it's probably curving back down, where it's getting at a low point at a ketogenic diet, is: Because the body can then start, being in ketosis, to burn off this obesogenic chemicals.

[Tucker means that in this study, the high endpoint was a higher percentage of calories coming from fat, which results in the body producing more ketone bodies]

Dr. Saladino:

Ah, that's so interesting: So if you exclusively feed animals polyunsaturated fatty acids, they go into ketosis and it burns off the HNE?

Goodrich:

Right. Still, there's one little problem with that: In excess, these fats are acutely toxic. They did a couple of human experiments, where they fed people a lot of polyunsaturated fats to try to get them into ketosis - and they all got nausea.

And nausea is a sign that you're eating a toxin, essentially.

Dr. Saladino:

It makes sense, yeah.

I've talked on previous podcasts with Thomas DeLauer about studies with ketosis, where they ate more or less polyunsaturated fatty acids. In those studies, it's messing up the metabolism. That's obviously a negative thing for humans. I'll leave it there, without getting too far down the rabbit hole.

Goodrich:

Just to kind of put the cherry on top of that point: There was a great study that I put on my blog years ago, where they looked at a high polyunsaturated fat diet in rodents.

They were lean, they didn't get obese and everything looked great, until they looked at their livers - and they were all suffering from massive liver failure!

So they were fit and ripped, but dying from the inside out. In the context of America suffering from a massive epidemic of liver disease, that only started in in the 1980s.

Dr. Saladino:

Yeah. Maybe this is a good time to talk about this one publication.

There's one study that comes up when people are trying to defend polyunsaturated fatty acids. And it's this muffin study from Sweden, do you guys remember this one?

Nobbs, Goodrich:

Yes.

Dr. Saladino:

With overfeeding... I can pull up the study and get your thoughts on it. This study gets brought up a lot, so it's worth addressing why we think this study is potentially problematic.

> *Overeating Saturated Fat Promotes Fatty Liver and*
> *Ceramides Compared With Polyunsaturated Fat:*
> *A Randomized Trial*

Goodrich:

Yeah, so there's two problems with the muffin study: The first is, we have no idea what these people were eating. If you would like to scrape the bottom of the barrel of nutrition science, this is the paper that you'd find.

Because the only component - that we know of for sure - of what these people are eating is the muffins, that's all that's described. And they're *excess* muffins, right?

So they're eating a 100% of their calories as *we have no idea what* - and then, they're getting extra calories as muffins. Which are carbohydrates, and then one of the two investigated fats.

Now, the fat that they're using isn't butter, they're using palm oil. By our crowd, palm oil is generally thought of being a healthy fat, because it's pretty low in omega-6 fats.

But here, we have to get into these issues of the structure of the fat. You don't eat fats, you eat triglycerides which is a glycerol molecule with 3 fats hanging off of it. 58

And it turns out that how those fats are arranged on the glycerol backbone matters! They've done studies with this in human infants.

Because when you get breast milk, you have a lot of saturated fat in the form of palmitic fat which is named for palm oil. It's in the middle position, and then the other two fats are something else.

In palm, oil it's reversed: The middle fat is something else and you have palm oil on the other, outer positions. It's like a fork: With palm

54

oil, the outer tines are palm oil - in breast milk, the inner tine is palm oil. [Palmitic fat]

That makes a big difference - in human infants, they can't digest palm oil! And it's recommended against using palm oil in formula, for the reason that it makes kids sick.

Now back to the muffins study:

To feed a fat that we know to be unhealthy in humans to a bunch of humans, where we don't know anything about their diet, except that they're eating muffins to excess... so here are the two problems:

1) We know eating too much is bad for you, regardless of what you're eating
2) We know that eating palm oil can be bad for you, because it's not a fat that we evolved to expect in our diet in such large quantities.

So this study doesn't really tell you anything, unfortunately. The people who ate the polyunsaturated fat muffins did do a little bit better, okay. But, point 3:

We don't know if you had put them on an evolutionarily appropriate human diet, would this make a difference then?

I mean, as we talked about before:

There are populations that they've looked at where people overeat seasonally. We humans are supposed to have a lot of fat on us, often more than we would like. And we overeat seasonally, to put fat on so that when we get to the dry season or to winter, we have enough fat to make it through.

This is a not a helpful study, let's just put it that way.

Dr. Saladino:

(...)

Yeah, regarding palm oil: There are huge palm farms about 30 to 40 miles from where I live, and I think „Why are we making all this palm oil?!"

Again, it's a processed food. These are refineries to make this palm oil. Humans would never have been exposed to this. And interesting that it's not allowed in in formula, because it makes infants nauseous.

Goodrich:

It turns into soap in your gut!

Dr. Saladino:

Wow! The other thing you mentioned about this muffin study is that this is an overfeeding study. Which is kind of a strange thing to use it as a pro-seed oil study.

As you said, there are populations that overeat seasonally. But they forced people to gain weight in this study. I think that the goal was a 3% weight gain. They were making people overeat to gain a certain amount of weight.

These were muffins baked with palm oil or muffins baked with seed oils. They just had to keep eating muffins until they gained that weight.

So the people who are anti saturated fat / pro seed oils will look at the study and say

„Haha, look! When the people overate the the seed oil muffins, they did better than when they overate the palm oil muffins!" But to me, it's just like:

„What is the model that we're using here? In what nutritional universe are we thinking that stuffing people literally beyond their point of satiety, until they gain a lot of weight, is representative of normal life?"

Goodrich:

Well, this is also their best piece of evidence, which is hilarious! Because it gets back to our discussion:

They say „Oh, seed oils are good! They don't make you fat!" - and we look at the United States, where seed oil consumption has gone up steadily - and we're in the middle of a massive epidemic of obesity! And other related diseases.

We get back to „Okay. Well, how much of this stuff exactly do we have to eat before we start getting healthy again?"

We know that if we don't eat any of it, we're healthy! And these guys, I guess, are telling us that if we eat massive amounts of it, we'll get healthy.

Even though from the animal studies, we know that it'll give us liver failure. Which they don't like to talk about.

Dr. Saladino:

The animal literature is very clear. No one could defend any sort of animal literature in favour of seed oils. These oils look extremely bad in animal studies.

Goodrich:

That's the reason why the proponents of seed oils don't like to use them.

Dr. Saladino:

Yes, exactly. The reason we're having this podcast is because we don't have the studies that we would prefer to have in humans. Studies that really put the nail in the coffin. So we have to come at it from different angles and think about it in other ways.

Goodrich:

We do! At least for obesity. You know, we've talked about HNE... which is one of the big thrusts of the article because that's one of the obesogenic mechanisms of seed oils.

The other big mechanism where we do have human data is the endocannabinoid system.

Dr. Saladino:

Let's talk about that.

Goodrich:

Yeah, so endocannabinoids are these chemicals that were originally discovered in marijuana. Hence the name, cannabis. And endocannabinoid is a cannabis-like molecule that's made in your body.

Everybody has at least heard of the effect called *the munchies*, where you get stoned and it makes you want to eat. And from what I've been told, you don't crave steak - you crave junk food!

Now, this effect is so well described, that THC (the exocannabinoid in pot that makes you get the munchies) is actually an FDA approved drug called Dronabinol. Which is used in cancer patients and people with AIDS who have a problem with a lack of an appetite.

You give them synthetic THC, Dronabinol, and it makes them want to eat. So that's a great thing for them.

In your body, you have this process where arachidonic acid, an omega 6 fat, is turned into endo-cannabinoids in your gut! And these endocannabinoids...

If you want to make your body to make endocannabinoids and stimulate a hunger signal, the easiest way to do it is to not eat. And your body's reaction to fasting is to make these chemicals that make you hungry and make you want to eat. Right? That's perfectly normal.

If you eat excess linoleic acid, then your body has more of the building blocks for these endocannabinoids. Because it converts linoleic acid to arachidonic acid to these hypophagic endocannabinoids. *Hypophagic* meaning they make you eat too much.

We know that process, it's well described in animal models.

It's so well described in animal models, that we had a drug to treat it - called Rimonabant. Rimonabant was introduced in the 2000s, it was considered a miracle drug!

Interestingly, to get to our other white papers:

Not only does it nearly eliminate obesity in animals and humans, but in humans it also improves all the cardiovascular and diabetic risk factors! So it makes everything look better. It even lowers your HbA1c.

So it was a miracle drug - and it works because it blocks the endo-cannabinoid receptors in your brain and in your gut. Thus, it stops you from wanting to overeat from the production of these chemicals.

Unfortunately, in humans... and this is a good caveat on these animal models:

Apparently, the rodents they were using didn't have the opportunity to kill themselves. Because that's what Rimonabant made people who took the drug want to do. Commit suicide! So it was pulled from the market.i

But it worked, it was effective and it was considered a miracle drug, until they figured out this negative side effect of it.

So coming for a different angle now: One of the most effective treatments for obesity in humans (and in animals) is gastric bypass surgery. The most effective one we have there is Roux-en-Y gastric bypass, RYGB.

This RYGB surgery, when it's effective...

And it doesn't work about 20% of the time, it also makes lots of people who got it want to kill themselves. Thus, the suicide rates are very high, so it's not a recommended way to cure your obesity, in my opinion.

But when it works, it works! Because you're basically cutting the signal between the brain and the gut that enables this endocannabinoid pathway. And all of a sudden, you stop craving junk food!

THC, if you inject it into the brain of a rodent, makes them want to eat sweet and starchy foods. Just like in humans. If you block this pathway, people spontaneously start avoiding junk food and eating healthier foods. That's one of the reasons why it helps people to lose weight, when it works.

I keep saying that because I want to make the point that it only works about 80% of the time. These surgeries are not a precise science and they're still trying to figure out exactly what nerves you need to cut, to have that effect on the body.

The other problem with this surgery is that sometimes people grow their guts back! The gut is an amazingly resilient organ and it seems that in some cases, people start growing new receptors for these fats along the gut, and the effect can wear off after a while and the obesity comes back.

But in animal models, this surgery has the same effect as Rimonabant. What's really fascinating is that if you take animals that have had this surgery and you give them these endocannabinoids, it partially blocks the effects of the surgery and they start getting fat again.

Dr. Saladino:

This is super interesting! Here you can see a picture of how they do a Roux-en-Y gastric bypass:

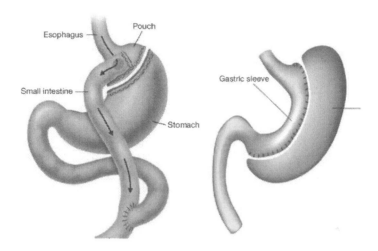

They essentially reroute where the stomach connects, by taking the esophagus, cutting the stomach, and then attaching this sort of blind pouch lower in the process.

Goodrich:

That upper part of the small intestine that they bypass is where these fat receptors are. That's where the process of making these endocannabinoids happens.

Dr. Saladino:

What we're doing is: We are bypassing part of the small intestine - and how interesting that this decreases these endogenous cannabinoids being created. And sometimes, I guess, then people will re-grow receptors down in the lower part of the ilium or something, Tucker?

Goodrich:

Yeah, the gut's pretty amazing. I mean, I had a colon resection years ago. You would think cutting 8 inches out of your colon would have a negative impact. But in two and a half days, I was out at a pool party, drinking beer and eating hamburgers - on the doctor's advice!

It's unbelievable how capable your gut is of healing. Which makes sense, because that's one of the things in your body where if it doesn't work, you're not gonna last for very long! It has amazing powers of healing.

But despite all my caveats about this surgery - when it works, it's miraculous. The miracle for these people is that they lose this massive craving to overeat. And it's happening because of this welldescribed mechanism that endocannabinoids control your stimulus to overeat.

Now, how does that work? Because they've done a lot of research on this and we go through all of it in the blog post.

They've done some experiments in animals, trying to figure out *what's driving this?* What we know is not driving this, is carbohydrates and protein - has no effect on this pathway. How much fat you eat has an effect on it - depending on the omega-3 and the omega-6 fat components in the diet. Okay.

Why are the omega-3s important? Because if you eat omega-3 fats along with your omega-6 fats, they take precedence in the gut and **they replace the omega-6 fats**. So you're not producing as much of these endocannabinoids.

Meaning, with more omega 3 fats, you're not stuffing your gut full of omega-6 arachidonic acid - which is turned into these endocannabinoids that make you overeat. That's an important point.

Nobbs:

Tucker, can I just double down on what you said? Because I think it's so important, I'll try to do a very short version, just to to hammer it home here:

THC gives us the munchies, uncontroversially smoking marijuana gives us the munchies.

There are also cannabinoids within our body, endocannabinoids, like 2AG and AEA, and that also stimulate these CB1 receptors [Cannabinoid receptor type 1] the way that THC does. It's the activation of CB1 receptors that makes us hungry.

And increased linoleic acid intake in our diet increases to 2AG and AEA, which increases the stimulation of CB1. This has been shown very clearly in rodent studies.

Interestingly, in a follow-up to that study in mice, showing that increased linoleic acid led to increased endocannabinoids, which led to weight gain and increased hunger... they also did a separate study where they fed salmon increased amounts of high linoleic acid meals...

Goodrich:

...and soybeans.

Nobbs:

...and soybeans, yep. By doing that, the salmon had higher amounts of linoleic acid in their fat, their flesh.

Then fed they fed the salmon that ate high linoleic diets to a group of mice. And they fed different salmon that was lower in linoleic acid to a different group of mice.

And the mice that ate the salmon that ate the higher linoleic acid diet actually gained more weight!

So if this is an indication for humans, it means: If we're eating chickens and pigs that had the high linoleic acid diet - even if we're doing everything else right, that could still lead to weight gain!

But back to the the THC, the 2AG and AEA with CB1 activation story, carrying that over to humans:

These studies with Rimonabant that Tucker mentioned, that *is* how it works! It's not like *1 of 50 ways of how it works and this is one little byproduct*. No, that is why it is found to be such a miracle drug.

And then when you look at bariatric surgery or gastric bypass, again, it is the CB1 receptor, theblocking or the lowering of CB1 activation in the gut - that is why it works. There are papers on this, we're not making this up. It's very clear!

And then just to highlight one other point that Tucker touched on: If you directly administer the endocannabinoid AEA - which is one of those endocannabinoids that is increased with linoleic acid consumption - that reduces the fat loss of gastric bypass surgery. Which points to that it is the same mechanism at play there.

- All of the things that increase your appetite, like THC, and
- All the things that really help us lose weight, like bariatric surgery, and
- Drugs like Rimonabant

they're all working on the same pathway here. And that same pathway is activated when we increase our consumption of linoleic acid!

Dr. Saladino:

So, reiterating what you both said: If you decrease your consumption of seed oils, you decrease the formation of endocannabinoids in the gut - and you are less hungry! It's great that you brought this up, Jeff. People just hate it when I talk about this:

But this is one of the reasons why I have concerns about chicken fat and pork fat, from animals fed corn and soy - because those are going to have way too much linoleic acid in their fat.

We know this, I've spoken about it on previous podcasts. You can look at wild chickens, wild pigs or wild hogs, they have 4 to 5% linoleic acid in their fat.

But when you look at conventionally raised chickens and pigs, they have 16 to 25% linoleic acid in their fat! Perhaps even more. I did a podcast with Brad Marshall about this.

It all has to do with how appropriate the diet given to these animals is. And though there are people now who are raising low PUFA (Polyunsaturated), low linoleic acid pork, they have to be very intentional about what they're feeding the pigs. I've never come across a chicken farm that is able to do that.

Maybe you guys are aware of some. I have friends that have experimented with chicken feeding and gotten the linoleic acid in their eggs down. But it's one of the concerns I have about eating tons of eggs and tons of chicken fat.

Goodrich:

Well, there's to make you feel a little bit better about that, as I was describing saturated fat and palm oil, there's a similar phenomenon going on in chickens:

A lot of the linoleic acid is apparently attached to phospholipids, rather than triglycerides. There's some evidence suggesting that the damaging form of linoleic acid is when it's coming in a triglyceride, not in a phospholipid. The body processes it a little differently.

The same is true for omega-3 fats. Why is fish better than fish oil? Because in fish, you're getting the omega-3 fats as triglycerides and also as phospholipids - and in fish oil, you're only getting the triglyceride format! Your body needs both.

Dr. Saladino:

Right, and I would imagine there are phospholipid-derived omega 3s in animal fats as well. Butter or grass-fed beef having phospholipid forms of omega-3s.

Is there a way that you're aware of Tucker, that they can modify whether the linoleic acid is in a triglyceride versus a phospholipid, with what these chickens or pegs are fed? Do you think that that makes the bacon and chicken fat less problematic than seed oils?

Goodrich:

...no. I mean, as Jeff described, even the best case for that would be salmon! And Jeff described that study where even salmon which have a high level of omega-3 fats, even when they're farm raised compared to a chicken or a pig, still wound up being obesogenic to the animals that were fed them.

I think ultimately, the best way to keep linoleic acid as triglycerides out of your body is **to eat as little of it as you can!**

Nobbs:

One of my takeaways is... You know, we're only two whitepapers in, we could probably write 10 more! Actually, we are planning to write many more, whether it's about insulin resistance or the effect of different foods on brain health, Alzheimer's, dementia, cancer, etc.

Linoleic acid plays a role in all of these!

And something like the *phospholipid form versus triglyceride form* may have an impact on one or two of those. Maybe it results in fewer instances of cancer or doesn't have as big of an impact on dementia. But it may have just as big of an impact. And it seems to, on something like obesity and weight gain. So it's hard to just pinpoint if that makes it all better.

And Paul, to your point on chickens. This could actually be an area where I would align with the conventional wisdom of:

If you're going to eat a chicken, you should eat the chicken breast, not the chicken thigh!

Dr. Saladino:
Right!

Nobbs:
Chicken thigh is unquestionably more delicious but chicken breast is better because it's low fat. And this is the case where actually being low fat - when you're eating something like chicken or a pig - could be the way to go.

Goodrich:
...or putting your bacon on paper towels to absorb the excess fat...

Dr. Saladino:
...and not cooking in the bacon fat...

Nobbs:
Yeah. I mean, it's got upwards of 30% PUFAs - it's more than canola oil!

The video of how you make it maybe would be less disturbing. Or not, depending on where you stand. But I have a restaurant chain - and for years, we're actually looking for chicken that we could put on the menu that wasn't wasn't fed corn and soy.

I can't tell you how many farms we talked to. Even farms that have regeneratively raised chicken. And - there isn't any! Maybe there's like one or two farmers who have 12 chickens, that sort of thing

But to actually buy any sort of scale chickens that aren't fed high linoleic grains, I don't think it exists. At least not in the US.

Goodrich:
I had a farmer I used to buy pasture raised chickens from and I could go visit them and watch them run around in the field. They were delicious but they were like $40 a bird! It would not scale up.

Dr. Saladino:
Yeah, that's cost prohibitive to get that kind of food.

Okay. So one of the other white papers at Zero Acres is the linoleic acid or the *seed oils and cardiovascular disease* posts. This one is excellent as well. I want to talk about this, let's just hit on some of the high points of this post. 68

Because this is also really interesting: A lot of people who don't believe what we're saying about seed oils will say „There's no evidence that seed oils are inflammatory."

When I look at the number of the references that you guys share in this seed oils and cardiovascular disease post... I remember our previous conversation Tucker and I think *how could you possibly think that seed oils are not inflammatory?*

When they clearly raise
- Oxidized LDL
- LP(a)
- CRP
- Oxylipins and .
- Oxysterols.

But I'll let you guys give us a perspective, what do we know here?

Goodrich:
Well, there's a basic distinction between these two posts: The seed oils cause obesity post - although there's excellent support for it in the scientific literature - is kind of revolutionary.

Even a lot of the experts seem to be oblivious to the evidence about the endocannabinoid system controlling food intake.

The exact opposite is true of the cardiovascular disease post!

There is literally **no other explanation** in the literature for what causes cardiovascular disease, than the progression from linoleic acid to oxidized linoleic acid metabolites in the body, initiating and causing the progression of heart disease.

I mean, there's a paper that came out recently:

> *Low density lipoproteins cause atherosclerotic cardiovascular disease.*

This is a consensus statement from the European Atherosclerosis Society, and it's got some of the most revered scientists in this field.

If you read it closely, when they get to these steps that are required to initiate cardiovascular disease, the very first step is the oxidation of linoleic acid in LDL - which converts it from nonatherogenic LDL to atherogenic oxidized LDL!

They reference a study that was done back in the late 1980s. Where they actually concluded that line of research, by feeding people (first rabbits and then people) either olive oil or seed oils, and then measuring the susceptibility of their LDL to oxidation.

In this study, it was clear that in humans, the amount of seed oils you consume predisposes your LDL to oxidation - which is the required step to initiate atherosclerosis. And there's been lots of studies done showing this exact same thing.

So that's a fundamental difference between those two posts: We are pointing something out that they have been saying, privately, in the journals for decades. There is no other explanation for what causes cardiovascular disease.

As this article does, they will say „Oh, it's LDL" - but it's not LDL! It's only LDL when you have oxidized omega-6 fats in the LDL. That is the required alteration in LDL to make it atherogenic.

Dr. Saladino:
That's such an important point. I go round and round in my mind... with physicians who will not have discussions with me about LDL and atherosclerosis.

Prominent physicians, who discuss the lipid hypothesis and the idea that *more LDL is always bad* or *more LDL is worse.* They say apoB is essentially the same measure of LDL because there are only a few apoB containing lipoproteins.

But they say „More LDL is bad, all the time. If your LDL goes up, no matter what else you're doing in your life, you should take a Statin!" That drives me bonkers and I don't understand why these physicians won't have a conversation with me.

This is a really, really important point to note that not all LDL is created equally.

To just say that *more LDL is bad,* without

- any sort of qualification of the oxidation status of that LDL
- someone's underlying insulin resistance, which will also impact how oxidized that LDL is, and
- the health of the arterial wall

is ludicrous and myopic to me.

In the post that you guys have on Zero Acre, you also note experiments with macrophages.

Essentially, within the arterial wall (beneath the endothelium) these immune cells, these macrophages live.

And most people would agree that the beginning of atherosclerosis or plaque formation is a fatty streak. Even before that happens, we get these foam cells, correct me if I'm saying any of this wrong, guys.

These foam cells are macrophages taking up LDL. But they're not just taking up any LDL! Because when they've done the experiments, the macrophages will not ingest native LDL that is not oxidized.

That LDL must be oxidized, there must be something that triggers this macrophage receptor to take up an oxidized LDL particle. Again: Macrophages will not ingest native LDL, LDL must be oxidized to begin the formation of foam cells.

And here we have the hypothesis - or perhaps it's even beyond that, a mechanism:

1) More linoleic acid in the human diet increases the amount of linoleic acid in the LDL particle

2) If there's more linoleic acid in the LDL particle, that LDL is more susceptible to oxidation

3) We know that oxidation is a prerequisite for the formation of foam cells, which are the beginning of atherosclerosis.

Did I get all that right? I mean, what am I missing here? How can people not see this?

Goodrich:

That's exactly right, and that was demonstrated by the gentlemen who discovered the LDL receptor and got a Nobel Prize for it, back in the 1980s: Brown and Goldstein.

The first thing that they tried to do after establishing this pathway existed, was to take some macrophages and incubate them with LDL, then wait for the foam cells to appear - and it failed.

So two other scientists, Steinberg and Witztum, were the guys who finally figured out „Oh, it's the seed oils! And they have to be oxidized, then we can make all the foam cells that you want!"

That's the paper that the European Atherosclerosis Society references as „This is the first step." There's no other explanation.

Nobbs:

It seems very clear when you actually look at the data. I think Paul, to answer your question about „How can people not see this?"

I think the reason is because this is how things evolve, especially in nutrition science. It's always one broad category. Like fat, right?

• Fat is bad and carbohydrates are good.

Then there's an evolution of that understanding.

- Oh, there are different types of fat. Like saturated, monoun-saturated and polyunsaturated.

Then for a while,

- Polyunsaturated fats were just good.

Before we even understood that there were omega-3 fats and omega-6 fats.

And now, there's at least more of an understanding that

- Omega-3 seems to be protective, but omega-6 fats seem to be bad.

And it's the same for cholesterol:
- First, it was all about total blood cholesterol.
- Then there was an understanding of HDL and LDL.
- Now there's more of an understanding of oxidized LDL.

The same in other aspects, like trans fats. Broadly, there are trans fats, then there are things like CLA, trans fats in dairy, as well as trans fats from partial hydrogenation. Those are very different things.

These are just words that humans come up with to categorize these things. There's nothing in nature that says *these two are related in one way,* and *these two aren't related in that same way.* They're just the words we use to describe these things. But they're completely different molecules.

Different molecules have different effects in our body. So if this is like other aspects of nutrition, hopefully our understanding continues to evolve and become more nuanced and granular.

Where we understand that it's the oxidation of LDL, primarily through linoleic acid, that seems to be the real culprit here. And it does seem like we're going in that direction, as opposed to: Not that long ago 50, 60 years ago, where it was just broadly speaking choles-terol.

So we are continuing to get more and more refined. And as we do that, the argument for what causes heart disease is becoming very much aligned with the „We shouldn't be eating high linoleic acid seed oils"- argument.

Goodrich:
And we're getting back to the evolutionary argument. That these novel food products are causing the chronic disease. Which is exactly what you would expect if you have a system, a well-designed system like a human body, and it stops working.

Speaking as somebody with an engineering background: If I had a computer system that started misbehaving one day, the first thing I would look at was what changed on the inputs. And that's where nutrition science is finally getting, decades later „Oh gee, we started eating this stuff that we never ate before, and now we're sick. Oops!"

Nobbs:
Going back to the categories example I was using: At least we're starting to point the finger at processed foods. That that's a pretty recent phenomenon.

In the 1990s, the American Heart Association... I have a blog post actually showing their pamphlet on this subject, coming from Nina Teicholz.

They basically had a whole section about how you should eat low-fat cookies, hard candy, gumdrops and sugar - as long as you're replacing fat with those foods.

Goodrich:
Fruit Loops were a heart healthy food!

Nobbs:
Yeah, they may still even be.

Dr. Saladino:
Cheerios and Honey Nut Cheerios are!

Goodrich:
Well, we got aways from the sugar a bit, thanks to Gary Taubes.

Nobbs:
So it's only been a decade or two since we've understood that processed foods are no good. What will happen next? The next evolution will be „Wait! What is it about processed foods that make them bad?" And really, that's going to take us to refined flours, refined sugars and seed oils.

Then we'll probably have another decade of arguing about which is which. And then maybe in like the 2040s, we'll finally come to the conclusion, we'll Infiltrate the Zeitgeist and everyone will understand „Seed oils have got to go!"

Dr. Saladino:
Yeah. You know it's funny, I had my friend Tommy Wood on the podcast and we were talking about this. And he said that exact same thing about processed food. He said „Just look at processed food, that's pretty clearly a driver of chronic illness in humans."

Now, I also want to point out that there are a few people in the nutrition sphere on Twitter and otherwise, who don't necessarily believe that processed food is bad for humans and think it's just a pure calories thing.

That is a little bit ridiculous to me as well. But I love your perspective Jeff, and I share with you that when somebody like Tommy says "Okay processed foods are bad. I'm not satisfied by that! I want to know what component of the processing is harmful for humans," we have to go into more detail.

I don't include processed sugar in my diet. I don't include grains or processed grains in my diet. And I don't include seed oils. So I think that if you do those 3 things, you've pretty much got all the bases covered.

If you look at what processed foods are: They are processed grains, processed sugars and seed oils. If you eliminate those 3 things from your diet, you've got the basis covered.

Now, the problem becomes: Seed oils creep into a lot of foods that people think of as healthy. Like salad dressings, like chicken or like restaurant food.

That's a big deal, that's why it's important to drill down. Because people may not understand

Hey, this salad dressing with canola oil, soybean oil or sunflower seed oil is a problem for me. And is contributing to many of these issues that I have.

Furthermore, people may not even know what their food is cooked in - or what the foods they're eating are eating themselves! The chickens, the pigs, the salmon. I think it's super important that we inform the public about these things, these nuances.

Goodrich:

That was exactly where I started: I ate a ,healthy diet', I ate in accordance with the Dietary Guidelines for the most part.

I was literally at the end of the salad bar, when I looked at all the squeeze bottles of salad dressings and said „That's got to be the cheapest oil known to man - to make it into my office cafeteria!"

I was in fact eating a healthy diet - and yet, I was sick! And just making that one change changed everything for me. I mean, 14 years of chronic irritable bowel syndrome ended in two days! And it came from eating ,healthy things' like polyunsaturated fats rich salad dressings.

Dr. Saladino:

Is that why you had to have your bowel resection, Tucker? I wanted to ask you about that so everyone understands the full story.

Goodrich:

I had acute diverticulitis which is one of the classic diseases of civilization. And I can reproduce the symptoms, for me personally, with

69

wheat and vegetable oils. I'm extremely gluten intolerant. I don't know how much that affects other people, but there are clear...

I mean, IBS alone: This is one of the areas where the epidemiology says that there are clear links between linoleic acid consumption and IBS, irritable bowel syndrome. There's a direct relationship between consumption and the disease.

So I don't know if that'll get you to a colon resection the way it did me, but it will definitely lead you to be ill.

Dr. Saladino:

Well, having acute diverticulitis with an abscess could get you a colon resection...

When I was writing *The Carnivore Code,* I thought it was really interesting looking at the literature for diverticulosis. Which is the formation of these sort of pouches in the colon that can become infected, that's called diverticulitis.

A lot of people would think „Oh, diverticulosis is you don't have enough fiber!" - but there's actually no literature to support that connection.

Goodrich:

Even worse: People who eat more fiber are more likely to have diverticulosis!

Dr. Saladino:

Yeah, and there's a large endoscopy study, I think with over 3 000 patients, that found that people who ate the most fiber had the most incidence of diverticulosis! Now, we can't say correlation is causation, but we certainly...

Goodrich:

There's also different kinds of fiber. I mean, we've spent all this time talking about how there are different types of fats, so there are also different types of fiber.

I wouldn't say fiber causes diverticulitis or diverticulosis. There is a whole range of issues with wheat as a human food, that are kind of outside the scope of this discussion right now.

Because the original work that they did is in Africa, where people who ate lots of fiber didn't have diverticulosis or diverticulitis. So I think it's fiber in the context of only an industrial diet and seed oils are playing a role there, leading to those diseases.

Dr. Saladino:

I wouldn't doubt that seed oils have some involvement in the formation of diverticulosis. The most interesting thing I found was that diverticulosis appeared to have an autoimmune component.

Because there are so many things that are autoimmune in nature that we don't think of as being autoimmune in nature. Whether it's

70

a mood disorder like depression or anxiety, heart disease or type 1 diabetes.

There's immunologic connections with all of these. Certainly, type 1 diabetes is clearly autoimmune. But diverticulosis may very well be autoimmune in nature. Then the question is: *What is triggering that autoimmunity?*

So thanks for sharing the story and bringing that full circle. Any closing remarks, anything we didn't talk about?

In one those white papers, I also found a bunch of literature you guys had noted on linoleic acid and age-related macular degeneration, that case is very strong.

If people are not aware of the connections between seed oil consumption, by proxy linolic acid, and age-related macular degeneration (or ophthalmologic eye problems), that case is very strong! And there's lots of evidence for that on the Zero Acre website, too.

Goodrich:

To be clear about what that means: Age-related macular degeneration is the leading cause of blindness in the United States!

So you would not be saying something crazy, if you said *linoleic acid is the leading cause of blindness in the United States*. That's how strong the evidence is.

Dr. Saladino:

There probably will be a reel on Instagram where I say exactly that, Tucker!

I'll let you guys each have a moment to kind of summarize this.

Nobbs:

So I would just say, let's not forget that we talk about some of these different diseases in a bit of a silo. Like

- Let's talk about heart disease
- Let's talk about obesity
- Let's talk about insulin resistance.

They're all related! There are terms that I think Paul inadvertently said earlier - like *Diabesety*. Where we actually have words now to describe the relationship between these things. 76

So something like high linoleic acid intake unquestionably being a cause of age-related macular degeneration, it probably doesn't stop there. And what it's doing to our eyeballs is probably also why it's related to skin health. What's happening on the inside of our bodies and what causes obesity.

There's plenty of research out there showing the links between obesity and heart disease, and diabetes or insulin resistance.

So there are randomized controlled trials - really well-designed ones - showing increased rates of different disease states like cardiovascular disease.

And while they may not measure something like insulin resistance or weight gain, we can probably infer that the group that had more cardiovascular disease wasn't doing so well when it came to insulin resistance and obesity as well.

The last thing I'll just say is: At the bottom of the ZeroAcre.com obesity post, we talk about „Well, what about the studies that show seed oils are good?" We talked about the muffin study, there are a handful of reasons why there's a lot of conflicting evidence here.

When you really look into it, they don't seem all that conflicting.

- One is the overreliance on observational studies
- One is studies looking at fresh soybean oil versus cooked soybean oil
- Another one is just the study duration.

If you're looking at *what happens for the next few hours* or even *for the next couple weeks...* it's just going to take longer than that to get really good data.

Aonther point I'll make is that there is really interesting data on how genetics dictate the rate at which each of our individual bodies convert linoleic acid to downstream metabolites!

So studies that show one person having low levels of linoleic acid in their body, and another person having high levels - those levels don't necessarily correlate to dietary linoleic acid intake.

And the person having lower levels of linoleic acid but worse health outcomes - it could be because their body was so quick at converting that linoleic acid into even more harmful molecules! So that may be very misleading.

Dr. Saladino:
This is in the plasma?

Nobbs: Yes, exactly. That's also a fascinating rabbit hole that you can go down through references on our blog post. But there are a lot of reasons why you should look beyond the abstract or the study title, when really looking into this stuff.

Dr. Saladino:
Yeah, I appreciate that. That was something I wanted to touch on, that studies looking at levels of linoleic acid in the blood are basically worthless. Because we don't know ALDH2, polymorphisms, aldehyde dehydrogenase, these type of enzymatic systems that can convert linoleic acid to HNE. These can change.

72

Like you said Jeff, if people have lower amounts of linoleic acid in the blood:

Is it that they're breaking it down to HNE at a higher rate? And if they have higher amounts of linoleic acid in the blood, are they breaking it down to HNE less? It's just not a good measure.

You can let me know if you agree with this, I think that adipose linoleic acid is a better metric of consumption, but it's difficult to assay that.

Goodrich:

It's a metric of long-term consumption, absolutely.

Let me put it this way: Having had this long conversation between the three of us about the dangers of linoleic acid, to reiterate the point Jeff just made:

Linoleic acid itself is probably harmless. It's the stuff it turns into in your body! Every part of this obesity post is   Well, it turns into HNE - that's toxic.

It turns into arachidonic acid, which turns into these endocannabinoids - which make you overeat.

It's always a couple of steps away from linoleic acid. So when you see a study that says... for instance, the inflammation paper, saying *We looked at biomarkers of linoleic acid intake, linoleic acid in the blood.*

We've got decades of research, showing that another linoleic acid biomarker, oxidized LDL, is central to the process of cardiovascular disease, which is an inflammatory process!

Dr. Saladino:

Alright! So where can people find you guys if they want to read more about this? We talked about ZeroAcre.com, the blog posts are amazing, the white papers are amazing.

Nobbs:

More info on me, well, ZeroAcre.com is a good place to start. Because I've been kind of pouring all of my waking hours into that over the last few years.

But I also write on a number of different topics at JeffKnobbs.com Mostly focused on health and nutrition and a lot of the stuff that we talked about today. Putting a lot of data behind the things that people tend to not put data behind.

I'm on Twitter, but haven't been tweeting too much. And Tucker and I have written a number of those blog posts together at ZeroAcre.com.

Goodrich:

Yeah, so what Jeff just said: He's also got some great posts on his personal blog, by the way. Getting into some other issues like the environment that aren't really covered anywhere else in the health community. But I think are very important.

So yeah, I'm involved in the Zero Acre posts that are coming out... My blog is Yelling-Stop.Blogspot.com I've been doing a YouTube series of interviews lately, under my name Tucker Goodrich.

I'm also active on Twitter, my handle is @TuckerGoodrich

I just want to thank Jeff for putting all this effort into this, he's really turbocharging getting this message out. And it's super important that somebody's doing this, that people are committed to getting this information out. It's been really terrific!

Dr. Saladino:

Yeah, I appreciate you guys both massively. I look forward to the day that I walk into a fast food restaurant and I ask

„What kind of oil do you use in your fryer?" and they say

„This cultured oil from this place called Zero Acre!" and I go

„F*ck yeah, that's cool!"

Nobbs:

Shout out to Mesley, a new restaurant in San Francisco that is doing just that - they're the first restaurant to start frying with cultured oil!

Goodrich:

Wasn't there a McKinsey conference, where they were serving Zero Acre Cultured Oil?

Nobbs:

Yeah, we were surprised, they made a sesame dressing using cultured oil.

Dr. Saladino:

And just in case people were wondering, the cultured oil from Zero Acre is how much linoleic acid? Two percent?

Nobbs:

Every batch is a little different. But it's 2. something, always less than 3 percent. So yeah, if you add oil and fat to your food, go eat low linoleic fats and oils, people!

Dr. Saladino:

That's the key! Thank you both, I think we're probably gonna have to do a part two. Thanks for all your work!

Both:

Thank you, Paul!

Chapter 3

Interview with Dr. Chris Knobbe:

Are seed oils to blame for diabetes, heart attacks and chronic disease?

Minute 13:55

Knobbe:

How about Metabolic Syndrome? Metabolic Syndrome was described once in 1921 and in the 1940s. 1981 was really when this took on its current meeting, it was described by Hanefield and Leonard in 1981.

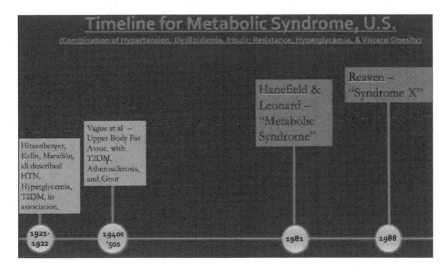

And Reaven in 1988 called this "Syndrome X". This is a condition of insulin resistance, visceral adiposity, abnormal lipids, hypertension, and... what am I leaving out Paul?

Saladino:

Waist to hip ratio, low HDL, high triglycerides... Yeah.

Knobbe:

There we go. Okay. So in 1988, Metabolic Syndrome - from the NHANES 3 study - was 24%. 1999 to 2006, NHANES 4, it was 34.1%. 2006: Adults with Metabolic Syndrome from the international diabetes federation was 40%.

And 2009 to 2016? What we now know is 88% of adults do not meet five criteria of metabolic health.

If you look a their

- Blood glucose
- Triglycerides
- HDL
- Blood pressure, and their
- Waist circumference.

88 percent. And, as you know Paul (and probably most of the audience knows) that Kraft's research back from 1970 to 1999 showed, that 80 of americans had insulin resistance, based on his studies by 1990. 80 percent!

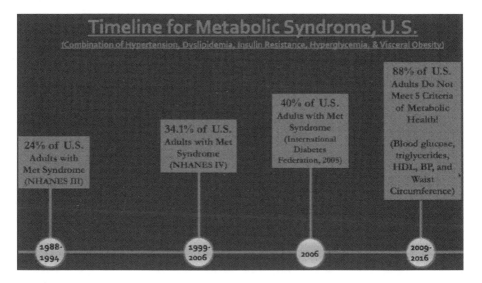

Saladino:

I spoke about that study, or that set of studies, with Ivor Cummins on a recent podcast. If you look at the data from the Euro Aspire Study, which Ivor and I talked about, it was exactly the same thing. That:

When people were admitted for heart attacks, there was a subset, maybe 20 or 30% that had known diabetes. And when they looked a little further, there was another group, another 20 to 30 percent, that had dysglycemia when they actually did the labs. And there was another group, another 20 to 30 percent, that had impaired postprandial glucose when they fed them sugar and failed oral glucose tolerance tests!

So when people were admitted for heart attacks, for cardiovascular disease in the Euro Aspire Study, only about a third were known diabetics. But when they looked for evidence of this Metabolic Syndrome, this dysglycemia, this perturbed handling of insulin and glucose... 80 to 90% of people had it!

Which is consistent with that 88% number of us adults don't get As in all five categories. Blood glucose, triglycerides, Hdl, blood pressure and waist circumference. And I've cited that study a bunch of times!

That 88% number is crazy to think about, and it's going to be relevant to this podcast and so many more podcasts that I will do. Especially the one upcoming on LDL with Spencer Nadolsky because we have to consider how...

If 88% of the population in the United States has some degree of metabolic dysfunction, could that skew the results we're looking at our studies? So that's something for the future you guys, think about it.

This history that you're presenting for us, Chris, is just staggering. If any of you guys want to be amazed, go back and watch this on Youtube and watch the video.

But, you know, your most striking slide that you've shown so far Chris was the first one, with publications from Harvard and Tufts... like you said, that say verbatim "No need to fear omega-6 fatty acids" and these are the *healthy* oils, canola oil... and they show people pouring those oils into a pan!

I just want to make very clear to everyone, is either: We are right or they are right. But one of us is very, very wrong! And these two views cannot coexist, we are taking a stand that is diametrically opposed to what the mainstream is saying. And looking at all of this really surprising history that Chris is showing us, is saying:

Even though the dietary guidelines came out in 1980, we got fatter after that and our and we increased 250 calories a day - we were already, at that point, getting much fatter since the early 1900s. And so the question that you and I love to both ask is: What the heck is driving this?

Yeah it really puts things in perspective, you cannot ignore these statistics.

Knobbe:

Right. I know that Ivor Cummins has made a strong argument that insulin resistance itself is driving all of this. But from my perspective, I like to go back further and say Well, what's driving the insulin resistance?" And from my perspective, I think it's primarily seed oils. I think that is the big picture.

Knobbe:

Back to the arthritis, I just want to tell you that the whole reason I ended up in this space, in nutrition, is my own arthritis started. It for me at age 33 or 34!

And it was... when I was 50 years old, almost a decade ago, that I changed my diet and drastically improved my arthritis. The reason I threw this in here because a lot of people are struggling with arthritis. It's huge! This has a lot to do with your diet.

59:50

Saladino:

This one is interesting, because you mentioned the adipose tissue concentration of linoleic acid in the Tokelauens, and that it was 3.8%. And this is a cool study that I found, looking at the adipose tissue concentration of linoleic acid in a study of Westerners:

Can linoleic acid contribute to coronary artery disease?[1-3]

Jonathan M Hodgson, Mark L. Wahlqvist, John A Boxall, and Nicholas D Balazs

ABSTRACT The adipose tissue concentration of linoleic acid was positively associated with the degree of coronary artery disease (CAD) in a cross-sectional study of 226 patients undergoing coronary angiography. Linoleic acid concentration in adipose tissue is known to reflect the intake of this fatty acid. These results are therefore indicative of a positive relationship between linoleic acid intake and CAD. The platelet linoleic acid concentration was also positively associated with CAD. After confounding factors were allowed for, the eicosapentaenoic acid concentration in platelets was inversely associated with CAD for men, and the docosapentaenoic acid concentration in platelets was inversely associated with CAD for women; results consistent with several other studies that suggest that fish, and ω-3 fatty acids derived from fish and fish oils, can beneficially influence macrovascular disease. *Am J Clin Nutr* 1993;58:228–34.

KEY WORDS Linoleic acid, ω-3 fatty acids, polyunsaturated fatty acids, coronary artery disease, atherosclerosis

Introduction

Many studies have examined the relationships between diet and end points of coronary heart disease (CHD) such as angina, myocardial infarction, sudden death, angiographically assessed coronary artery disease (CAD), and coronary mortality. The

been an associated reduction in total mortality. In England and Wales where minimal changes in this ratio occurred, there were also minimal changes in coronary mortality (7). However, not all studies have produced results that would indicate a protective role for linoleic acid. In a study by Blankenhorn et al (8) it was found that increased intake of linoleic acid significantly increased the risk of new atherosclerotic lesions in human coronary arteries.

Evidence for an inverse association between the long-chain ω-3 fatty acids or fish intake and CHD has been accumulating. A reduction in total mortality was demonstrated in a secondary prevention intervention study in which the intervention was fatty fish (9). Prospective studies have found an inverse association between fish intake and CHD incidence (10, 11), although an inverse association has not been demonstrated in all prospective studies (12, 13). Fish intake has also been associated with improved arterial wall characteristics (14). In a study in which platelet fatty acids were measured, eicosapentaenoic acid (20:5n–3) was inversely associated with angina pectoris and docosapentaenoic acid (22:5n–3) was inversely associated with risk of acute myocardial infarction. Also in this study, adipose tissue docosahexaenoic acid (22:6n–3) was inversely associated with acute myocardial infarction (6).

In our study the fatty acids in adipose tissue and platelets were measured. The relationships between each of the fatty acids and the degree of angiographically assessed CAD were examined.

Slide 1

It's a cross-sectional study of 226 patients - and there was a correlation between the adipose tissue concentration of linoleic acid and coronary artery disease in these people. So, it's interesting,

> "...these results are therefore indicative of a positive relationship between linoleic acid intake and coronary artery disease."

Again, this is observational epidemiology. This is cross-sectional. But what I want to point out is that very rarely do researchers look at the adipose tissue concentration of linoleic acid. Our detractors... the other side of the argument, from people who think that what we're talking about is nonsense, would be:

If you look at serum levels of linoleic acid, they don't correlate with adverse events. But adipose tissue levels of linoleic acid seem to! And so there's a real discordance here. The only thing I can take away from this, or what I conclude from this is:

Serum levels of linoleic acid probably are not a great indicator, long term, of overall linoleic acid consumption. Presumably, because some of that linoleic acid can become oxidized into the oxylipids which we're going to talk about a little bit in this podcast. I talked about it previously with Tucker Goodrich on this podcast.

But if linoleic acid gets oxidized into 4-HNE, and 9- and 13HODE, then you're going to see less linoleic acid in the blood. So serum, or plasma levels of linoleic acid are probably not good correlates for chronic illness. Serum levels are probably just not not good correlates for consumption, but adipose tissue levels are!

That's what Stephan Guyenet's research suggests, that adipose tissue levels are rising. There's tons of research that shows: The more linoleic acid you consume, the more linoleic acid ends up in your LDL particles - which is your 'bad 'cholesterol - and in your adipose tissue.

So, if you guys see people arguing, or offering a counterpoint (as they should), to what Chris and I are talking about and they're using serum levels of linoleic acid - we know those are probably not a good reflection. But if you look at adipose tissue levels, those actually do correlate with coronary artery disease... in this small study of 226 people.

That's, I think, a fascinating point that I just wanted to add as a counterpoint. And there's a couple other things we'll get to soon.

I'll hand it over back to you Chris.

Knobbe:
Okay! Those are great points. Again, we're back at this, this is where I believe we need to be with our linoleic acid.

We were at 9.1% linoleic acid in our adipose tissue in 1959 - and 21.5% in 2008. (...)

Then this is Stephan Guyenet's carb intake versus obesity prevalence. When our carbs dropped off beginning in 1999, when people started talking about going low carb, why did our obesity continue to increase?

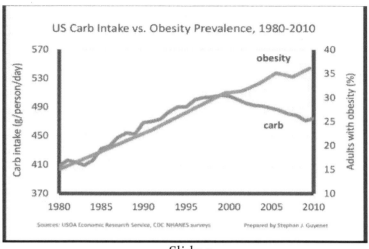

Slide 2

Carbs went down... and this is not consumption, this is total food available. Which is why you see that the carbs were so high, like 500 plus grams a day... which, you know, nobody quite eats that much. This is total food available. But it dropped down to something like 470, 480 grams a day by 2010 - while obesity continued to climb.

It's even more pronounced with sugar! By about 1998 or 99, somewhere in there, our sugar consumption: We started to learn that sugar is bad. Everybody knows sugar is bad now. And sugar has come way down, this is grams per person per day.

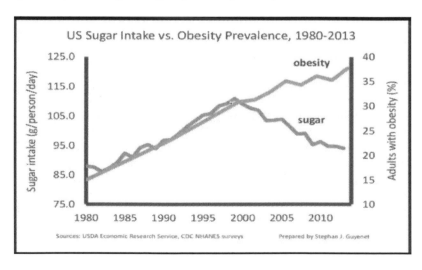

By 1999, I think, is when we hit the peak, so this is around 110 grams per person per day. And by 2000... wherever this ends 2012 or so, we're down to like 95 grams a day. Yet, again, obesity continues to climb!

This is a graph of seed oils versus type 2 diabetes in the United States that came that Cate Shanahan shared with me. I think this is in her book... but she's a colleague that Paul and I work with, and she shared this graph with me.

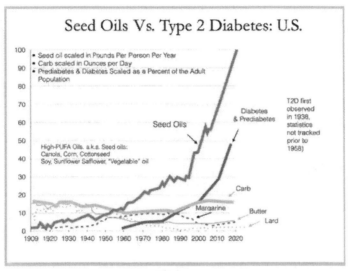

Slide 3

You can see the remarkable correlation between seed oils and diabetes and pre-diabetes - which has gone, as we reviewed, from 0.97% in 1960 up to... (well, this is both diabetes and pre-diabetes), so you can see they're almost at 50% today. This ends about 2018, right? So again, another remarkable correlation.

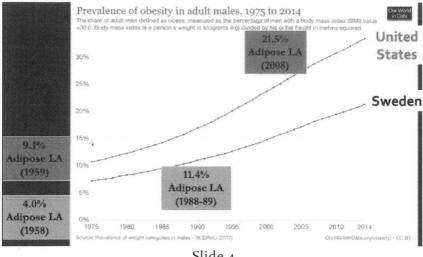

Slide 4

This is one of the things I was getting at, that I wanted to show everybody. This is a prevalence of obesity in males between 1975 and 2014. And I've plotted on here, again, our adipose linoleic acid. But this is pretty interesting, this is one of the only other adipose linoleic acid I could find. This happens to be in a developed nation, Sweden:

In 1958, their adipose linoleic acid was 4%! It was down there, close to the Tokelauens, right? But we don't have any obesity data going back that far - the first data begins in 1975 and their obesity was like 7%. So it was far lower lower than ours was in 1960. Right? Again, correlates with their adipose LA.

And by 1988 and '89, their adipose LA has upped to 11.4% and look what's happened with their obesity: It went from about 7% in 1975 up to about 22%! So it more than tripled in this period, between 1975 and 2014... and those are the only two adipose pieces of data that I have for Sweden:

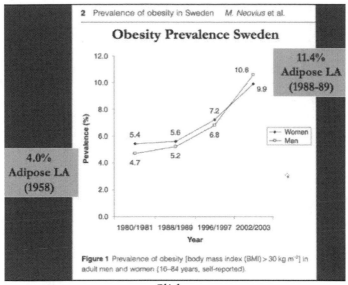

Slide 5

But here it is, this is overall prevalence of obesity, this is men and women both. Once again, this is just from 1980 to 2002, and you see that their obesity doubled. Again, correlating with their adipose linoleic acid increase.

Then this is young men 18 year old males. Again, we only have data beginning with their obesity in 1971, but their obesity was 0.9%! Their adipose LA in 1958, 4% - and look at their obesity in 1995, 3.2%!

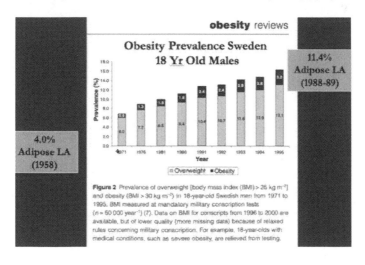

Obesity is the black number for those who can see this small data. And once again, with their rising adipose linoleic acid... I mean, you just just can't make this up...

(...)

Regarding carbohydrates and chronic disease: I think you could take all of the Asians... but let's talk about the Japanese because the Japanese is a huge population, it's like 130 million people. Let's talk about what's happened with them in the last 70 years.

So here we, are everybody knows Japan's one of the healthiest nations. Let's talk about how we know that.

In 1976: Men obesity rate was 0.7 %,women 1.5%. By 2014... by the way, this is obesity BMI 30 or higher. They changed that more recently because of the fact that Asians are normally so much leaner than us. So they changed obesity now - which they sometimes called *pre-obesity* - to a BMI of 25 and above.

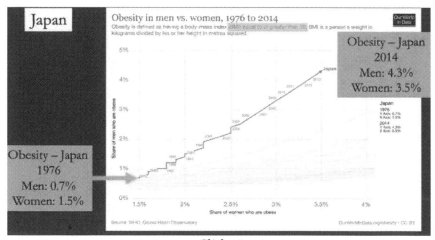

Slide 6

But nevertheless, for this study men for example went from obesity 0.7% to 4.3% - so this is like a 7-fold increase by 2013. In women, it wasn't nearly as much, their obesity approximately doubled.

So let's go back here and talk about their health, though. Now this Ancel Keys in famous... or is should I call it infamous, Paul?

His *six countries studie* of heart disease.

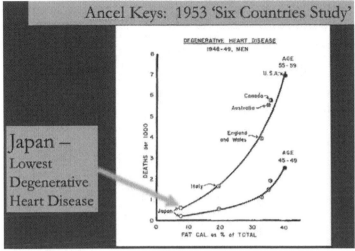

Slide 7

The reason I'm showing it is: He didn't make up this data, Japan was among the lowest of all nations, this was degenerative heart disease. So it's kind of a broad category. But the same category was used for all of these

Even in 1957, when Yerushalmy and Hilboe looked all the 22 countries... and, as we all know, the relationship that Keys presented sort of fell apart.

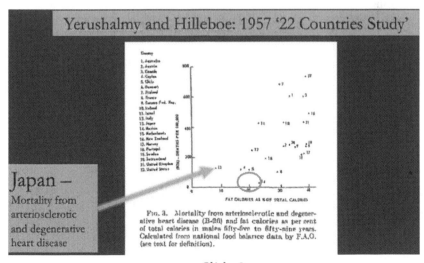

Slide 8

But Japan - I want to point out - still, among 22 countries, fell amongst the very lowest in terms of arteriosclerotic and degenerative heart disease. And they remain there today, actually! They're very, very low in comparison to developed nations. Number 14 [Marked] over here was Mexico. This is complicated but Mexico was probably not anywhere near that low in their heart disease at that time. Okay, so this is really interesting because... You know, once once World War II ended, Japan was in a devastated state - and we Americans occupied Japan beginning in 1945.

When you start looking at data of the late 1940s and 50s, things weren't very good there. You know, people will make arguments about what's going on with their diet at that point - and those may be well-founded. But here's what happened:

This is trends in nutritional intake this is really interesting: So from 1958 to 1999 their calorie consumption... 1958, they had all the food they could want they wanted and their calories were 2837 in 1958. And they went down to 2202 by 1999.

Journal of Epidemiology

Japan

Vol. 15, No. 3 May 2005

Table 1. Time trend in total daily energy intake and percent energy intake from fat, carbohydrate, and protein.

	Calendar year				
	1958	1977	1982	1989	1999
Energy (kcal)	2837	2243	2215	2205	2202
Protein (%)	11	13	13	16	18
Fat (%)	5	13	15	22	20
Carbohydrates (%)	84	74	72	62	62

Results are presented as mean values or percentages.

Table 2. Time trends in food intake (g/day).

	Calendar year				
	1958	1977	1982	1989	1999
Rice	593	299	290	232	236
Meats	1	31	45	74	72
Fish and Shellfish	56	95	97	105	71
Milk	13	31	45	74	99

Results are presented as mean values.

J Epidemiol. 2005;15(3):85-89.

Slide 9

The carbohydrate intake in percentage of total daily energy decreased markedly from 84% in 1958 to 62% in 1999! And I'm going to come back and show you this.

They had large increases in their protein intake, from 11% to 18%, and fat intake: Which was 5% in 1958, 20& in 1999

Look at their carb consumption: 1958, 84% - and this is almost all refined white rice. And each decade, their carb consumption went down, from 84% all the way to 62% by 1999. Okay?

Look at their rice consumption: 593 grams a day in 1958, 236 grams a day in 1999. Okay? So their carbs are going down, down, down.

What about their health? Look at what happened in the exact same time frame: Their diastolic blood pressure went from 73.5 to 82, hypertensive medications 1958: 3% - but 20% took those in 1999. Their BMI went from 21.7 to 23.7 in the same time frame. Their smoking went down from 68.5% to 45.2%.

▌Japan ▌

Table 3. Time trends in coronary risk factors.

	Calendar year				
	1958	1977	1982	1989	1999
Total cholesterol (mg/dL)	152.5	160.9	177.5	189.7	194.2
Systolic blood pressure (mmHg)	132.9	128.8	133.2	131.0	131.6
Diastolic blood pressure (mmHg)	73.5	76.3	81.6	79.7	82.0
Hypertensive medication (%)	3	4	5	7	20
Body mass index (kg/m²)	21.7	22.7	23.0	23.3	23.7
Smoking rate (%)	68.5	68.9	62.0	57.5	45.2

Results are presented as mean values or percentages.

What about diabetes? Just between 1997 and 2007, 6.9 to 8.9 million cases of diabetes - this was a 61% increase! And these authors say

"...the prevalence of type 2 diabetes in Japanese population is not dramatically lower than in a Western population."

As we know, Paul, the Asians are particularly prone to Metabolic Syndrome with our diet

Here's another one, this paper *The global spread of type 2 diabetes in children and adolescents.*

Here's what they say:

"The incidence of type 2 diabetes mellitus among Japanese primary school children in Tokyo increased 10-fold, from 0.2 per 100,000 in 1976 to 2 per 100,000 in 1995."

"In junior high school children, the reported incidence of type 2 diabetes in 1995 was 13.9 per 100,000, almost twice that of 1976."

And here's what they found in Okinawa:

*"The prevalence of Metabolic Syndrome was 30.2% in men and
10.3% in women [in 2003 -2004-]." and
"...half of the men aged over 40 are obese." - in Okinawa*

That's with a BMI greater than 25.

This is a study about breast cancer. I'm just going to get right to
the graph and I'll show you that cancers of the breast, colon, lung
and rectum in Japan all markedly increased. They went up somewhere in the range of like 1.5 to 2.

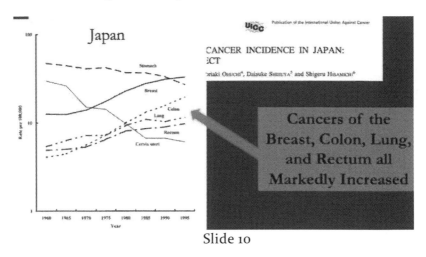

Slide 10

Now, you can see that their stomach cancer and their cervical cancer went down, and I don't really know the reason for that. I know
they had a suggested explanation for that but I really don't know
what that is.

But here, back to obesity in Japan. This is what they say, this is
from the Asia Pacific Journal 2002:

*"Obesity has become a public health problem in Japan. The national
nutrition survey of 2000 showed the prevalence of: Preobese males:
24.5%, and 17.8% in females. And Obese: 2.3% of males, and 3.4%
in females."*

So this is what's happened to them in this 40-year period, here's
the graph.

88

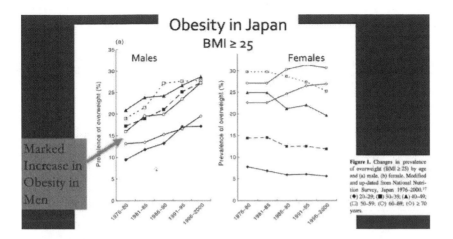

Figure 1. Changes in prevalence of overweight (BMI ≥ 25) by age and (a) male, (b) female. Modified and up-dated from National Nutrition Survey, Japan 1976-2000.[77] (♦) 20-29; (■) 30-39; (▲) 40-49; (□) 50-59; (○) 60-69; (◇) ≥ 70 years.

So you can see that there's a marked increase in obesity for all the age categories in males, the females not so much. They've remained pretty flat over this period, between 1976 and 2000.

This is a study where they monitor the trends of obesity in Japan. Take a look: This is men overweight and obese which is a BMI greater than 25, between 1980 and 2012.

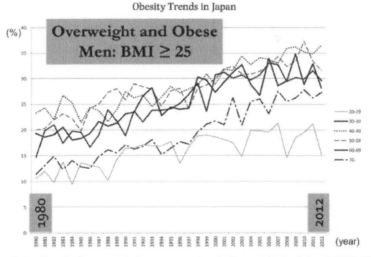

Fig. 2-1.   Trends of overweight by age group (men). Overweight (and obese): BMI≧25.
J Nutr Sci Vitaminol, 61, 847-819, 2015

Slide 11

You'll see that for every single category (these are broken up by decades), men in their 20s, 30s, 40s, 50s, 60s and 70s and beyond. All obesity going up.

Now this is the shocker: Here's their calorie intake for 1997 to 2011 and I'll put these two together:

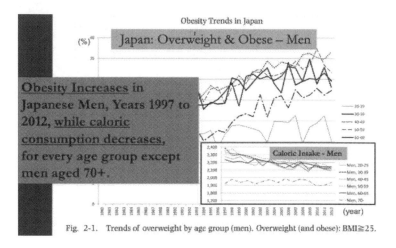

Fig. 2-1. Trends of overweight by age group (men). Overweight (and obese): BMI≧25.

Their calorie intakes are going down in all categories with the exception of men 70 plus... during the same period that their obesity is going up! So you can't even argue it's about calories. This is what we see in experimental studies.

This is our published data which regarded macular degeneration. Look at the vegetable oils. Again, we know 9 grams a day 1961 (their seed oils) - and that was at 39 grams a day by 2004. A 4.5-fold increase. Their sugar was going up you know until about 1970.

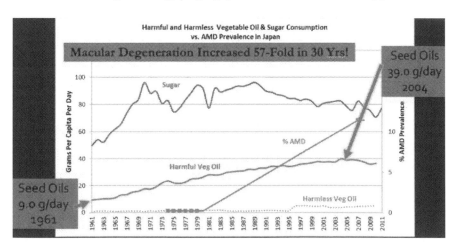

And then it's kind of leveled off between about 1970, and actually start going down around 1990. So it's been going down ever since, their sugar consumption... again, during the same time frame that their obesity is going up. By the way, their macular degeneration in this 30-year period between the late 1970s and 2007 went up **57-fold**

So here's some some interesting stats.

- With American occupation of Japan beginning after the war, this is the first time they got bread and milk in their school lunches. Never had that, just interesting.
- The first time they ever had hamburgers and cheese... not that those are anything wrong with, but it was the late 1940s.
- Their first fast-food restaurant in Japan was a Kentucky Fried Chicken, 1970.
- First McDonald's in Japan, 1971.

This is an interesting quote, I just had to throw it in here: So McDonald 1971, McDonald's Japanese partners named Dan Fujita said this:

"The reason Japanese people are so short and have yellow skins is that they have eaten nothing but fish and rice for 2 000 years." That's a pretty powerful statement.

Saladino:

Uhm, Yeah.

Knobbe:

So by 2007, in 36 years, there's now 3826 McDonald's - and 2012 there's 1120 Kentucky Fried Chickens.

Saladino:

And you know, those McDonald's and Kentucky Fried Chickens are not using beef tallow. They're using vegetable oils, seed oils, to make the french fries and the chicken. Just throw that in there.

Knobbe:

Of course they are because they were told, back in the 80s, that vegetable oils were good! The center for science of public interest, the SPI, told them back in the 80s "You've got to quit using that beef tallow to cook your french fries in, you got to cook it in vegetable oil. It's healthy!" Right?

(...)

Look at look at this data, this is fast food sales.

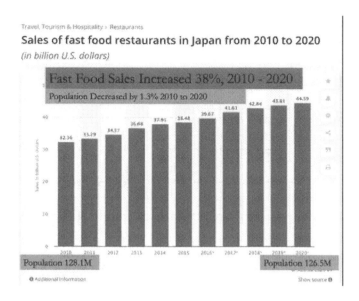

Sales of fast food restaurants in Japan from 2010 to 2020

(in billion U.S. dollars)

Fast Food Sales Increased 38%, 2010 - 2020

Population Decreased by 1.3% 2010 to 2020

Population 128.1M

Population 126.5M

I wish I had this going way back. But we know that there was no fast food in Japan until 1971. None in Japan, none!

But here they are, between 2010 and 2020 their fast food sales increased 38% in this last decade. At the same time their population decreased by 1.3%.

This is their population in 2010 [left side] 128.1 million and here it is in 2020, 126.5 million. They're having fewer kids, so their population is actually going down.

Here's kind of the wrap up on just Japan and then I'm going to talk about Okinawa, too. So Japan carb consumption:

1958, it was 84%. 1999, it was 62%. Their fat consumption went from 5% in 1958 to 20 % in 1999.

Japan Dietary History		
Japan	**1958**	**1999**
Carb. Consumption	84%	62%
Fat Consumption	5%	20%
High PUFA Oils	9 grams/capita/day (1961)	39 g/capita/day (2004)

So if carbs are bad and fat is good... their fat went up 4-fold in this period and their carbs went down about 20, 25%. Why are they getting sick?

But: Their high PUFA oils went from 9 grams a day in 1961 to 39 grams a day in 2004.

Saladino:

And you mentioned earlier that they're eating less calories. This is an interesting trend because in the United States we see, that as you mentioned earlier in the podcast, that we are consuming about 250 more calories per day than we were in the 1960s. So some some who would argue with us would say "No, no. The main problem is that humans are eating more and moving less."

Well, we certainly are eating 250 calories per day more. Now, the question, as I talked about with Tucker Goodrich in that podcast, was why? And one of the reasons may be... or one of the hypotheses for that may be that high omega-6 oils - these high pufa oils, this linoleic acid - might be sabotaging our satiety mechanisms and leading to more consumption of calories.

But Japan is really the the interesting mirror for this and puts it all in perspective over these similar years. They're eating less calories, gaining more weight, getting more sick eating less carbs and eating more linoleic acid!

And as you said earlier in the podcast: Something has to correlate if you're going to infer causation - and the carbohydrate consumption doesn't correlate. Calorie consumption doesn't even correlate. But polyunsaturated fatty acid oil does, especially!

If you're going to claim or suggest a correlation, it has to correlate. This really disqualifies a lot of things. And I think it clarifies the carbohydrate issue...

And, again, just to kind of put this in perspective for people: I don't think Chris or I is advocating for a 62% carbohydrate diet. But what I've said in my messaging recently is...

I get a lot of emails from people at *HeartandSoil.co* who are doing strictly hardcore carnivore diets, and I did that for a long time in the beginning. And a lot of people who are on strictly ketogenic diets, very low carb diets or strictly hardcore carnivore diets do sometimes develop electrolyte deficiencies.

You know what? Adding a small amount of the least toxic carbohydrates back to your diet solves that immediately. And I'm talking 50 to 100, maybe 120 grams of carbohydrates a day, from ancestrally consistent sources, as I've talked about in the past. It just changes your physiology in a way that makes an animal-based diet much more sustainable.

It doesn't have to be so dogmatic toward a nose-to-tail carnivore diet, a nose-to-tail animal-based diet with animal foods and the least toxic carbohydrates is so much more sustainable for most people. What we're illustrating here is:

Hey, a little bit of honey in your diet, a little bit of seasonal fruit - heck, even a little bit of white rice isn't going to kill you, as long as you're not overconsuming it in terms of calories.

Those are not going to hurt you. White rice, it has had the hull removed, you can pressure cook it. Not everybody does great with all the carbohydrates but there are less toxic sources of carbohydrates than corn flour, wheat flour, bread, you know... high fructose corn syrup and soda -which has essentially no satiety point associated with it and other problems in terms of the carbohydrates.

I think that things like beans and other grains, oats, quinoa are all problematic for humans. For whatever reason, when you pull the grain, or you pull the hull off rice, it seems to work for some people. It's not the only carbohydrate, there's also fruit and honey.

And we just want to clarify that there is some flexibility here in terms of the amount of carbohydrates. If you go too high in your car-bohydrates... you only have so many calories you can eat in a day! My problem with diets that are this high in carbohydrates, a 62% carbo-hydrate diet, is:

How are you going to get enough animal foods in your diet to get the micronutrients you need to thrive? I've talked about that before.

But that's why this is such an important point, that carb consump-tion calories... they don't even correlate with chronic disease in Ja-pan. It's such an interesting example here!

Knobbe:

Right, right. I really agree and I'm not advocating a 60 or 80% car-bohydrate diet either.

I'm not a low carber, I'm not a low fatter. I'm not a low protein guy - just low processed food, primarily.

Saladino:

Well, I bet you are a low carb guy, technically speaking, Chris. Be-cause we're talking about Western definitions of low carb... you could clarify this for me or we could look at the actual the actual definition.

But I believe it's anything less than 40% of your calories from car-bohydrates. So even when I eat

- a couple of oranges
- an apple a couple of tablespoons of honey, on dif-ferent days, or I have

- a cup or two of rice in a day, which are basically the only carbohydrates that I eat

I'm really not going to go much over 100 grams of carbohydrates, 400 calories out of what's probably a 2500 calorie day for me.

I'm well below 40% of my calories from carbohydrates. I am certainly low carb! And unless you're eating pasta - which I know you don't, I'm pretty sure - you're low carb as well

Maybe just not ketogenic which would be, you know, less than 50 grams of carbs a day. So I think you're probably a low carber but you don't know it.

Knobbe:
Well, I actually have been cycling carbs a bit. So there's weeks that I'm really low carb, and then there's weeks that I go much much higher carb. But again, overall, I just would agree with you, Paul, that it doesn't...

Refined white rice is certainly a nutrient deficient food. I think it's a staple carbohydrate for most people, but it's not going to provide hardly any nutrients.

1h:38

Knobbe:
Let's talk about the most famous Japanese region: Let's focus in on Okinawa which is the southernmost prefecture of Japan. It's an island, the city of Okinawa has something like 125,000 people, but the island itself I think has about 1.35 million people.

From this study, "Are they really that old?", they tell us here that they do possess the longest life expectancy and the lowest risk of age-related chronic diseases in Japan.

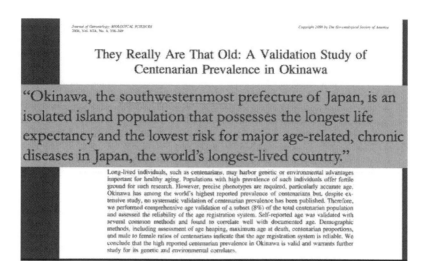

They Really Are That Old: A Validation Study of
Centenarian Prevalence in Okinawa

"Okinawa, the southwesternmost prefecture of Japan, is an isolated island population that possesses the longest life expectancy and the lowest risk for major age-related, chronic diseases in Japan, the world's longest-lived country."

Long-lived individuals, such as centenarians, may harbor genetic or environmental advantages important for healthy aging. Populations with high prevalence of such individuals offer fertile ground for such research. However, precise phenotypes are required, particularly accurate age. Okinawa has among the world's highest reported prevalence of centenarians but, despite extensive study, no systematic validation of centenarian prevalence has been published. Therefore, we performed comprehensive age validation of a subset (8%) of the total centenarian population and assessed the reliability of the age registration system. Self-reported age was validated with several common methods and found to correlate well with documented age. Demographic methods, including assessment of age heaping, maximum age at death, centenarian proportions, and male to female ratios of centenarians indicate that the age registration system is reliable. We conclude that the high reported centenarian prevalence in Okinawa is valid and warrants further study for its genetic and environmental correlates.

Slide 12

The world's longest lived country. So they do hold this - or did hold this - category between 1976 and 2004. They had 2644 total centenarians, here's the population of the city of Okinawa.

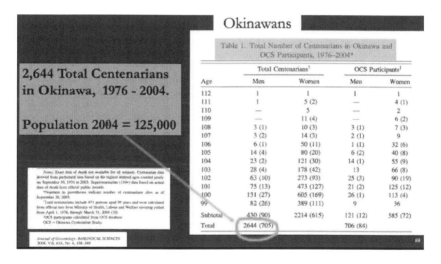

I think that's what they're drawing these centenarians from and not the whole island. But they do have a lot of centenarians.

These researchers, of course, they're always trying to figure this out. "What's driving this? Is it low calorie? Because they're eating nutrient dense, antioxidant rich, the low glycemic load?" They're trying to figure this out, right?

96

I want to show you some data here because this is pretty interesting.

Table 2. Estimated Nutrient Composition by Dietary Pattern

	Traditional Okinawa*	Modern Okinawa†
Carbohydrate (% kcal)	85%	58%
Protein (% kcal)	9%	15%
Fat (% kcal)	6%	27%
Sat. Fat (% kcal)	2%	7%
Cholesterol (mg/1000 kcal)	--	159 mg
Sodium (mg/d)	1113 mg	3711 mg
Potassium (mg/d)	5199 mg	2155 mg

Slide 13

So carbohydrate consumption in traditional Okinawa 85%. You know, nobody argues this. And modern Okinawa: 58%. Look at their fat percent, in traditional Okinawa 6% and now 27%.

Their saturated fat was 2%... *traditional* was back around 1950 - and now 7%. Now, the 7% saturated fat, this is where the American Heart Association is telling us today to have our saturated fat. Their saturated fat is still among... it's about the lowest of any developed nation in the world.

Okay, now in comparison, I just want to show: In the United States, our coronary heart disease is 6 to 12-fold worse than Okinawa. Our colon cancer: 2 to 3-fold greater. Our prostate cancer: 7-fold greater. Our breast cancer: 5-fold greater than Okinawa in 1995.

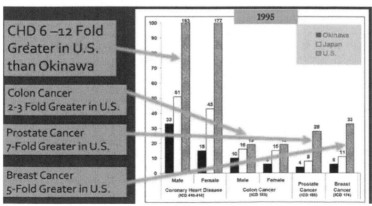

Slide 14

Just for comparison. This is a study, again, asking: Is it about caloric restriction? The diet of the world's longest-lived people, is this about caloric restriction?

Let me show you this data because I think this is very, very interesting. So here's Okinawa, 1949. Here's their carbohydrate consumption, 85%. Total fat 12 grams or 6% of their calories.

TABLE 1. Traditional dietary intake of Okinawans and other Japanese circa 1950

	Okinawa, 1949[a]	Japan, 1950[b]
Total calories	1785[c]	
Total weight (grams)	1262	**4.8 g Total**
Caloric density (calories/gram)	1.4	**PUFA!**
Total protein in grams (% total calories)	39 (9)	
Total carbohydrate in grams (% total calories)	382 (85)	**2.4% of Cal.!**
Total fat in grams (% total calories)	12 (6)	
Saturated fatty acid	3.7	
Monounsaturated fatty acid	3.6	
Polyunsaturated fatty acid	4.8	**~1.5% Om-6**
Total fiber (grams)	23	

85% Carbs, 1949!

7 — 12% Om-6 LA typical of "Westernized diets"

And here's what I wanted to show, ladies and gentlemen: Look at their polyunsaturated fat. This is omega-6 and omega-3 together:

4.8 grams! Okay? That's 2.4% of their calories. So what's that in omega-6? About 1.5%!

Again, I always want to compare: Here's a westernized diet, 7 to 12% omega-6. So they're down there in the same category, these Okinawa, as the Massai, as the Tokalauens, as the Kitabans, as the Papua New Guineans, of Tukasinta... on and on. They're all down at that level.

Here we go, Okinawa and Japan: Both 3 grams of oils a day in 1949, 1950. Three grams!

TABLE 1. Traditional dietary intake of Okinawans and other Japanese circa 1950		
	Okinawa, 1949[a]	Japan, 1950[b]
Food group	Weight in grams (% total calories)	
Grains		
Rice	154 (12)	328 (54)
Wheat, barley, and other grains	38 (7)	153 (24)
Nuts, seeds	<1 (<1)	<1 (<1)
Sugars	3 (<1)	8 (1)
Oils	3 (2)	3 (1)
Legumes (e.g., soy and other beans)	71 (6)	55 (3)
Fish	15 (1)	62 (4)
Meat (including poultry)	3 (<1)	11 (<1)

Okinawans consuming ONLY 3 Grams of oils/day, in 1949!

Americans consuming ~3 g/day in 1900, ~18 g/day in 1949, and 80g/day, 2010!

Just for comparison, Americans were consuming 3 grams of oil a day in 1900 - we're at 18 grams a day by 1949, and 80 grams a day by 2010! No wonder the Okinawans were so healthy, and the Japanese, back in 1949 , 1950.

Here we see the the the table on this. Again, showing their oils at 3 grams a day - which is 2% of their calories in Okinawa, 1 percent of calories in Japan.

TABLE 1. Traditional dietary intake of Okinawans and other Japanese circa 1950		
	Okinawa, 1949[a]	Japan, 1950[b]
Food group	Weight in grams (% total calories)	
Grains		
Rice	154 (12)	328 (54)
Wheat, barley, and other grains	38 (7)	153 (24)
Nuts, seeds	<1 (<1)	<1 (<1)
Sugars	3 (<1)	8 (1)
Oils	3 (2)	3 (1)
Legumes (e.g., soy and other beans)	71 (6)	55 (3)
Fish	15 (1)	62 (4)
Meat (including poultry)	3 (<1)	11 (<1)
Eggs	1 (<1)	7 (<1)
Dairy	<1 (<1)	8 (<1)
Vegetables		
Sweet potatoes	849 (69)	66 (3)

Sweet potatoes alone = 69% of calories in Okinawa, 1949!

Fruit	<1 (<1)	44 (1)
Seaweed	1 (<1)	3 (<1)
Pickled vegetables	0 (0)	42 (<1)
Foods: flavors & alcohol	7 (<1)	31 (2)

Sweet potatoes for Okinawa, 1949: 69 % of their calories. It was only 3% of calories in Japan because the Japanese were eating white rice. So the big point: Sweet potatoes alone accounted for 69% of calories in Okinawa in 1949.

Now, people are going to argue "Well it's because they were in post-World War II recovery." Let me come back to that and I'll show you that's not true.

Here's what happened to their sweet potatoes, they dropped them like a bomb, from 1950 to 1960.

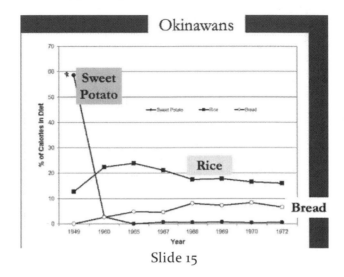

Slide 15

And their rice consumption and their bread consumption went up.

But here is the big deal, back to our study. Here I plugged in the oils. So agsin, seed oils 3 grams a day 1949, 9 grams a day by 1961. 39 grams a day by 2004 people. Probably people are sick of hearing me say, that but that's where they were.

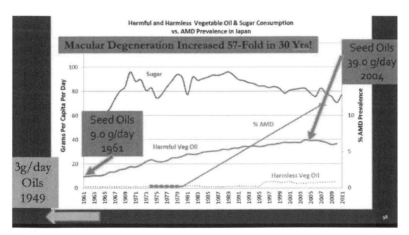

Here's all of the fast foods in Okinawa and I just counted, this is from 2020. 18 McDonald's in the city of Okinawa. Kentucky Fried Chicken, 10 of them. Remember, Okinawa is 125 000 population, at least the city - but they're just swarming in our fast food.

I showed this before, prevalence of Metabolic Syndromefor

Okinawans. 30.2% in men, 10.3 in women in 2003 and 2004

High Prevalence of Metabolic Syndrome among Men in Okinawa

Hideaki Tanaka[1], Takeshi Shimabukuro[1], and Michio Shimabukuro[2]

[1] Diabetes and Lifestyle-related disease Center, Tomishiro Chuo Hospital, Okinawa, Japan.
[2] Second Department of Internal Medicine, Faculty of Medicine, University of the Ryukyus, Okinawa, Japan.

The prevalence of metabolic syndrome was 30.2% in men and 10.3% in women [in Okinawa, 2003 – 2004]."

79 years, who underwent an annual physical chekup in our hospital between May

"... half of men aged over 40 years are obese (body mass index (BMI) ≥ 25)."

increase in the number of ATP III risk factors. Logistic regression analysis with the independent variables of sex, age, and HOMA-R gave an odds ratio of MS of 3.6 for men, 1.4 for a 10-year age increment, and 2.0 for an elevation of HOMA-R above 1.0. J Atheroscler Thromb, 2005; 12: 264–288.

Slide 16

And half the men over age 40 obese, in 2003 and 2004. Half of them obese! Here's some of their metabolic factors. Look at their BMI for Okinawans in 2004, 25.

- Triglycerides: Look how high they are, 156.
- HDL: In the men 51.9, really low.
- Look at their diastolic blood pressure, 82.
- Fasting glucose: Too high at 105.

Okinawans

Table 1. Demographic and Metabolic Characteristics of the Subjects.

Characteristic	Men (n = 3839)	Women (n = 3146)
Age (y)	49.2 ± 9.8***	50.0 ± 9.5
BMI (kg/m²)	25.0 ± 3.1***	23.2 ± 3.5
Abd.Circ (cm)	86.5 ± 8.1***	81.0 ± 9.3
TG (mg/dl)	156.3 ± 128.3***	97.4 ± 62.0
HDL-C (mg/dl)	51.9 ± 12.7***	61.5 ± 14.2
Systolic BP (mmHg)	130.1 ± 16.0***	123.2 ± 17.7
Diastolic BP (mmHg)	82.1 ± 10.4***	76.0 ± 10.9
Fasting glucose (mg/dl)	105.5 ± 24.0***	95.9 ± 14.5
HOMA-R	2.8 ± 2.0***	2.2 ± 1.6

BMI: body mass index, Abd.Circ: abdominal circumference, TG: triglycerides, HDL-C: high-density lipoprotein cholesterol, BP: blood pressure, HOMA-R: homeostasis model assessment ratio.
Mean ± SD, ***: $p < 0.001$ vs women (Student's unpaired t test)

And look at their homa IR, their in their insulin resistance: 2.8.

What should this be Paul? About 1.4? No more than that? **Saladino:**

Pretty low, yeah. You want it to be lower than that, yeah.

Knobbe:

Lower, okay. Paul, I pulled this up last time, this study from Okuyama, published in 2016. And he's on our side he knows this stuff. Here's his graph

We're back at looking at Japan total, the whole nation. Not just Okinawa in this study.

But look, anybody can see: Their caloric consumption has gone down since 1950, confirming what I showed you. Their carbohydrate consumption went way down. Their protein is stable for 60 years.

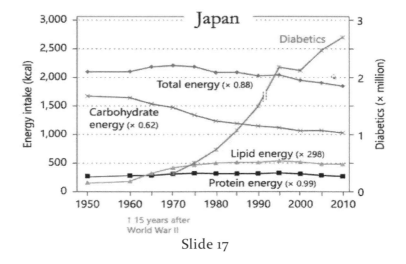

Slide 17

But what happened? Their lipids went up - and what were these lipids? That 39 grams of oils? And remember only 20% of their calories is fat. So guess what that means, paul? I mean, I haven't done the math but...

Like 40 grams is 360 calories... most of their fats coming from seed oils. This is astounding! And look what happened to their diabetes, this is the total number. But it was like 300 000 back here in 1970, and now they're at 2.7 million people with diabetes.

Here this is another comment, from another paper. This is from 2012

Comments on Dietary Restriction, Okinawa Diet and Longevity

Natalia S. Gavrilova   Leonid A. Gavrilov

Center on Aging, NORC and the University of Chicago, Chicago, Ill., USA

Gerontology. 2012;58:221-223.

> "Indeed, younger generations of Okinawans are losing their longevity advantage. We believe, however, that the most likely cause of this process is westernization of the diet in Okinawa rather than low caloric consumption of parents."

Slide 18

And they go on and say

> "Current demographic and nutritional data suggest that the remarkable Okinawan longevity is now a phenomenon of the past."

Of course it is, because they're consuming our seed oils. From a different paper, they say:

> "Okinawa has among the world's longest lived population. Recently this has begun to change. The life expectancy of men in Okinawa Prefecture fell to 26th from 4th among the 47 prefectures of Japan for the year 2000."

> "The nutrition transition in Okinawa with regards to increased fat intake and increased body weight were set in motion either directly or indirectly during U.S. administration, beginning in 1945."

They recognize this. You know, this is coming out of the Okinawan journal. They know that it's us, but they don't know that it's vegetable oils. Again, they're attributing it to fat!

(...)

I'm going to come back just for a moment to their obesity. I showed you this graph before. This is men's obesity going up since 1980 and the caloric intake for men is going down the whole time - with the exception of men 70 plus... Because older people tend to follow their traditional diets more.

Overweight and obese women: I don't know exactly why, but their obesity has been pretty stable. But their caloric intake has also gone down. I don't really have an answer yet for them and probably never will.

But here, I just plotted for overweight and obese men.

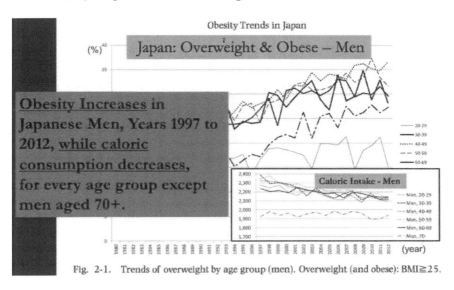

Fig. 2-1. Trends of overweight by age group (men). Overweight (and obese): BMI≧25.

This is the obesity up here at the top, going up. I plotted this year for year. So in the same exact years that their obesity is going up, their caloric intake for all categories - except men 70 plus - is going down! Now that is powerful, is it not?

Saladino:

You know, a moderate amount of vegetable oil is just a bomb metabolically for these people. The graphs might not look as as impressive as people were expecting, but when you actually look at the amount of calories coming from this linoleic and how much of a signaling molecule 10 to 20 grams of linoleic acid per day can be in humans - it's a big deal!

I mean, what we're talking about is the difference between 1.6, 1.8, 2% of your calories from linoleic acid - and 10% of your calories from linoleic acid. So we're talking about a 5x multiplier! But, that change... and even smaller than that.

In the first podcast that you and I did, we looked at some animal studies that showed that: Heck, at least in animal models, once you got beyond 5% linoleic acid, the damage had been done. I just think it's such an interesting idea that linoleic acid appears to be a very potent driver of these problems.

That's why it's important to understand your consumption of this. This is an interesting graphic which actually talks about the same thing. This is from the multiple risk factor intervention trial the MR FIT trial. These are the MR FIT quintiles. But here in this graph, this is coronary heart disease mortality and tissue highly unsaturated fatty acids [HUFA].

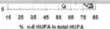

FIG. 1. Different tissue highly unsaturated fatty acid (HUFA) proportions among humans. The phospholipid fatty acids from 380 different plasma samples described in other studies from the United States (n = 294 [8]) and Japan (n = 87 [9]) were analyzed by gas chromatography. The proportions of individual n-3 HUFA decrease (○: EPA, 20:5n-3, ○: B: DHA, 22:6n-3, △: as the n-6 HUFA increase (▲: arachidonic acid (AA), 20:4n-6, △: B: di-homo-γ-linolenic acid (DGLA), 20:3n-6, □).

tial fatty acids are metabolized to different chain lengths [such as the 20-carbon arachidonic acid, AA (20:4n-6), and EPA (20:5n-3)] and stored as HUFA precursors esterified to tissue phospholipids from which they are mobilized by phospholipase-catalyzed hydrolysis (5). The closely related n-3 and n-6 essential fatty acids compete with each other for accumulation in tissue phospholipids, a process long recognized since the description of competitive hyperbolic interactions for these two types of nutrient by Mohrhauer and Holman (6,7). The voluntary food choices that people make day by day provide diverse proportions of n-6 and n-3 essential fatty acids associated with very different proportions of n-6 HUFA among the total HUFA of plasma phospholipids, which vary from 25 to 85% (Fig. 1). Competition between the n-6 and n-3 fatty acids is clearly evident in the decreased proportions of n-3 HUFA (DHA and EPA) associated with increased proportions of n-6 HUFA [AA and di-homo-γ-linolenic acid (DGLA)] that are stored in the tissue phospholipid HUFA.

High proportions of the n-6 precursor in the tissue HUFA that will be released during a stimulus will give high rates of formation of n-6 eicosanoids, whereas low proportions will give low rates of formation. In this way, the balance of n-3 and n-6 acids in the diet influences the balance of n-3 and n-6 HUFA in tissues and therefore the eventual balance of n-3 and n-6 eicosanoid actions in self-healing processes. CHD involves excessive n-6 eicosanoid actions in chronic and acute inflammatory processes in vascular walls that predispose people to fatal heart attacks as well as in the thrombosis and arrhythmia of the acute event. Because CHD is a major cause of death, many drug treatments are marketed vigorously to meet the need to treat people and reduce

an imminent risk. Figure 2 shows that the age-adjusted risk of CHD mortality is less when the proportion of n-6 eicosanoid precursors in people's tissue HUFA is lower. The wide diversity in abscissa values for Figures 1 and 2 raises the question, "What proportion of n-6 eicosanoid precursor is stored on the shelves of your body's medicine chest?" It also prompts a closer, more quantitative look at the association between tissue HUFA and CHD mortality.

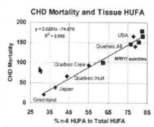

CHD Mortality and Tissue HUFA

$y = 3.0291x - 74.675$
$R^2 = 0.986$

FIG. 2. Coronary heart disease (CHD) mortality rates associated with tissue HUFA proportions. Results from the United States, Japan, and Greenland were discussed earlier (10, 11, 12) as were quintile results from the Multiple Risk Factor Intervention Trial (MRFIT) study ■ (13) and those from Quebec Inuit (14), Quebec Cree (15), and Quebec overall (16). For abbreviation see Figure 1.

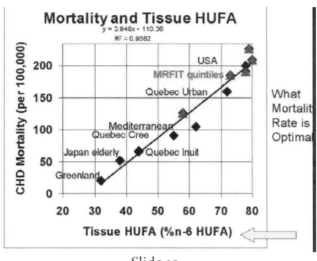

Slide 19

The x-axis here is the percent omega-6 highly unsaturated fatty acids in total highly unsaturated fatty acids. And again, this is tissue highly unsaturated fatty acid, so this is presumably adipose tissue.

You can see: The more omega 6 in the total polyunsaturated fatty acids, the higher the coronary heart disease mortality. Now, this is observational correlation - and I asked people on Twitter "Do you have any data that breaks this correlation?" I haven't seen anything from people. You can see Japan here, pretty low. I'd have to go back and look and see when these actual results were.

But you can see that the percent omega 6 as a percentage of your total polyunsaturated fats in your tissue correlates very strongly. **The r squared, the correlation coefficient, is 0.986** with the coronary heart disease mortality [!!!].

You can see Greenland here is very low, Japan, Quebec inuit, Quebec cree. And all of the MR FIT quintiles are up here on the top end. So I thought that was a striking correlation. This is from the paper "Diets could prevent many diseases." I wanted to share that one to correlate with that as well.

Knobbe:

Good one there! Anyway, here's the end result if you put all this together. You can see with Japan, the nutrition transition... and I created this graph. You can see their calories, you know from 1958 down down down... to From 2837 down to 1950 calories a day, in this 44 year period.

Japan – Nutrition Transition				
Year	1949 - 1950	1958 - 1961	1999	2004 - 2010
Total Calories	1916	2837	2202	~1950
Carb %	79	84	62	56
Fat %	8	5	20	27
Sat Fat %	2			7
Seed Oils (grams)	3	9	37	39
% Om-6 (of total calories)	~1.5	~1.0	~5.8	~6.2

- Carbohydrates: From 84% in 1958 down to 56%.
- Fat: 8% up to 20%.
- Saturated fat was 2% in 1950. We don't have any data until 2004. And their saturated fat was 7%

Here's their seed oils: They went from 3 grams a day to 39 grams a day -which is a 13-fold increase! And their omega-6 in 1949,1950 and 1960 was about 1.5 to 1%. And now, they are at 6.2% omega 6 in their fat.

1:57

Saladino:
I want to mention a few of the most impactful papers that I've seen here. Chris Ramsden's group is amazing! I think that this is the piece that you, Chris Knobbe... we will have to come back and talk about it more. I talked about this with Tucker Goodrich.

If you lower dietary linoleic acid in your diet, you are going to lower bioactive oxidized linoleic acid metabolites.

Slide 20

That's what this paper from Chris Ramsden's group is showing. There's no that you're going to lower these metabolites. And, if you had any question about those metabolites, the podcast with Tucker Goodrich is a great one to check out, until we complete this discussion.

And then, if you have any questions about the danger of linoleic acid oxidation products, things like this "*Unsaturated fatty acids and their oxidation products stimulate cd36 gene expression in human macrophages.*"

> Atherosclerosis. 2002 Sep;164(1):45-56. doi: 10.1016/s0021-9150(02)00046-1.

Unsaturated fatty acids and their oxidation products stimulate CD36 gene expression in human macrophages

Joan-Carles Vallvé [1], Katia Uliaque, Josefa Girona, Anna Cabré, Josep Ribalta, Mercedes Heras, Lluís Masana

Affiliations + expand
PMID: 12119192   DOI: 10.1016/s0021-9150(02)00046-1

Abstract

Fatty acids (FA) have been implicated in the control of expression of several atherosclerosis-related genes. Similarly, the CD36 receptor has recently been shown to play an important role in atherosclerosis and other pathologies. The aim of the present study was to evaluate the direct effect of FA and their oxidation products (aldehydes), on the expression of CD36 in both THP-1 macrophages and human monocyte-derived macrophages (HMDM). The FA tested included the saturated FA (SFA) lauric, myristic, palmitic and stearic acid; the monounsaturated FA oleic acid;

Slide 21

Well, CD36 is one of the receptors that's involved in the uptake of oxidized ldl and other problematic things in terms of the formation of a fatty streak, in the beginning of atherosclerosis.

So those two pieces that I just gave you guys are:
1) Decreasing linoleic acid in your diet will decrease linoleic acid oxidation products
2) Linoleic acid oxidation will trigger macrophages to take up more LDL, presumably.

This is an interesting study: "Low density lipoprotein rich in oleic acid is protective against oxidative modification."

PNAS

Proc Natl Acad Sci U S A. 1990 May; 87(10): 3894-3896.   PMCID: PMC54010
doi: 10.1073/pnas.87.10.3894   PMID: 2339129

Low density lipoprotein rich in oleic acid is protected against oxidative
modification: implications for dietary prevention of atherosclerosis.

Slide 22

In this study, they compared LDL oxidation of rabbits fed either a
high oleic acid sunflower oil (so that's high monounsaturated) versus
a high linoleic acid oil. Again, they didn't feed any tallow here, like I
wish they had.

But what they found was that when they fed the rabbits high
amounts of linoleic acid, the LDL that they pulled out - at least in
vitro in a test tube - was much more susceptible to oxidation. Hmm...
sounds like a very bad thing to me!

One of the last studies I'll show is just... there's been so much
pushback to these discussions... You know, I welcome the dialogue.
Unfortunately, not a lot of it has been respectful and there's a lot of
name calling. But, whatever.

But a lot of the pushback against what Chris and I are talking
about, like I said in the beginning of the podcast, is discussions that:
There are some studies out there that show that: If you give people
more linoleic acid, you don't see problems with increased oxidative
products of linoleic acid metabolism.

Chris kind of subtly addressed this earlier in the podcast, where
we talked about the fact that if everyone in a room is smoking, you're
in a dirty environment.

And if everyone in the population is eating more than 5% of their
calories in linoleic acid, and we believe that the cutoff point for human pathology is somewhere between 2 and 4%, then everyone is
already sick! And if you give them more than 5%, it is possible you're
not going to see an effect. That's the counter argument.

Now I just came across this study, fortuitously, in the last few
weeks. I thought it was so striking.. I don't know if you've seen this
one Chris, but what's so interesting about this group from Sweden
and Finland was:

When they look at the results of feeding people increased amounts
of linoleic acid in their diet, they'll do a run-in with increased saturated fat. So they kind of level the playing field.

In this study "A high linoleic acid diet increases oxidative stress in vivo in the body and affects nitric oxide metabolism in humans." They had 38 volunteers who consumed a baseline diet rich in saturated fatty acids for four weeks

Prostaglandins, Leukotrienes and Essential Fatty Acids (1998) 59(3), 229–233
© Harcourt Brace & Co. Ltd 1998

A high linoleic acid diet increases oxidative stress in vivo and affects nitric oxide metabolism in humans

A. M. Turpeinen,[1] S. Basu,[2] M. Mutanen[1]

[1]Department of Applied Chemistry and Microbiology, Division of Nutrition, University of Helsinki, Helsinki, Finland
[2]Department of Geriatrics, Uppsala University, Uppsala, Sweden

Slide 23

I love this experimental model, this is exactly what I would want to see. That they had a baseline of a diet rich in saturated fat. They took these people off of their high linoleic acid diets, presumably, what they were eating at baseline - and they put them on more saturated fat.

Then they switched them to a high linoleic acid diet 11.5% of energy, so way higher than what we would want - or a high oleic acid diet, 18% of energy, for four weeks. And they provided all of their food for the whole day.

"A controlled group of 13 subjects consumed their habitual diet throughout the study." This is essentially a control group study, there's no real placebo, but you get what I'm saying. Now, the results here are fascinating:

"The urinary excretion of 8-iso-PGF alpha," which is an oxidative product, "was significantly increased after the linoleic acid diet. Whereas the urinary concentration of nitric oxide metabolites decreased," that's a bad thing. Because you want to make nitric oxide for your blood vessels to be healthy! "No significant changes were seen in the oleic acid group." - which is what we would expect.

One of the problems we see here is that a linoleic acid is probably much worse than oleic acid. And there were significant differences between the linoleic acid group and the control group, for both the oxidative products of metabolism and nitric oxide. What's so interesting about this is that they say:

"In conclusion, the high linoleic acid diet increased oxidative stress and affected endothelial function, in a way which may in the long term *predispose to endothelial dysfunction."* - aka the precursors for cardiovascular disease. I just thought that was so cool that this group actually did a run-in with saturated fat and saw a very different outcome, than a lot of the other studies that are out there.

None of the people who would argue with us will show that study, Chris. but it looks like a pretty good study to me: They give people more linoleic acid, they have a saturated fat baseline, they actually try to simulate some sort of an ancestral diet - and they see increased markers of oxidation.

(...)

I think that we did a really good job in this podcast of talking about the history and the correlations. And really, like you said, showing people the whole movie. I don't really see how this is arguable.

Now, literature gets complicated and people can use studies to confuse. But if we look at the evolutionary history, if we look at the anthropology and we just look at the history of modernized countries and their intakes - it all becomes so clear!

Knobbe:

Yeah, yeah. If you look at, for example, Israel... and I'll just throw this out. We could dig into this, maybe, next time if you want to.

But Israel it should be the poster child for following Harvard's advice to consume vegetable oils, because they have higher vegetable oil consumption than almost anybody in the world... and their outcomes are devastating!

You know, if vegetables are healthy, then the people of Israel should be extremely healthy - and they are anything but!

Saladino:

Interesting! And I love what you said, this is an experiment that is being done on humans. We don't even know that it's being done.

I think in one of his papers, in that paper on linoleic acid metabolites, Chris Ramsden says the same thing. This is an unintended or unknowingly conducted experiment on humans that is completely evolutionarily inconsistent. These levels of linoleic acid, totally inconsistent.

And as I've spoken about before, there are lots of papers. I've shown this one before but I really can't show it enough.

Changes in Dietary Fat Intake Alter Plasma Levels of Oxidized Low-Density Lipoprotein and Lipoprotein(a)

Marja-Leena Silaste, Maire Rantala, Georg Alfthan, Antti Aro, Joseph L. Witztum,
Y. Antero Kesäniemi, Sohvi Hörkkö

Objective—To assess the effects of dietary modifications on oxidized low-density lipoprotein (LDL).
Methods and Results—Thirty-seven healthy women were fed two diets. Both diets contained a reduced amount of total and saturated fat. In addition, one diet was low in vegetables and the other was high in vegetables, berries, and fruit. The dietary intake of total fat was 70 g per day at baseline and decreased to 56 g (low-fat, low-vegetable diet) and to 59 g (low-fat, high-vegetable diet). The saturated fat intake decreased from 28 g to 20 g and to 19 g, and the amount of polyunsaturated fat intake increased from 11 g to 13 g and to 19 g (baseline; low-fat, low-vegetable; low-fat, high-vegetable; respectively). The amount of oxidized LDL in plasma was determined as the content of oxidized phospholipid per ApoB-100 using a monoclonal antibody EO6 (OxLDL-EO6). The median plasma OxLDL-EO6 increased by 27% ($P<0.01$) in response to the low-fat, low-vegetable diet and 19% ($P<0.01$) in response to the low-fat, high-vegetable diet. Also, the Lp(a) concentration was increased by 7% ($P<0.01$) and 9% ($P=0.01$), respectively.
Conclusion—Alterations in the dietary fat intake resulted in increased plasma concentrations of lipoprotein(a) and OxLDL-EO6. (*Arterioscler Thromb Vasc Biol.* 2004;24:498-503.)

Key Words: antioxidants ■ intervention ■ lipoprotein (a) ■ oxidized low-density lipoprotein ■ polyunsaturated fat

Slide 24

It's an interventional paper, where they decreased saturated fat intake by 10 grams a day and they increased polyunsaturated fat intake by 7 or 8 grams per day - and they saw an increase in oxidized LDL and lipoprotein(a).

I just feel like that's such a smoking gun: You decrease the fat that's supposed to harm you, saturated fat, and you increase linoleic acid... which Harvard and Tufts and all of these people are just pouring into pans, saying this is what's good for you. It's never something we would have had evolutionarily...

And you see LDL undergo changes that are clearly - most people would agree - are linked to the precursors of atherosclerosis.

So thank you so much for that, for going through all that in such detail, Chris. Where can people find more of your work or connect with you, if they want to talk about linoleic acid? Or eat coconut tortilla chips with you?

Knobbe:

You can come to our website Cure AMD Foundation, AMD for age related macular degeneration. Cureamd.org - you can just look me up on Youtube. I don't do a good job of trying to keep all those things in one place, but you can find find me on Youtube.

A lot of people have have gotten really interested in what I've been doing because of my Ancestral Health Symposium 2019 presentation, and my Low Carb Denver 2020, that was this this year.

One other thing: I just want to tell you Paul and all the listeners, that I was invited by Joe Mercola to collaborate on a book with him! And so we're gonna write a book together, we're working on it now actually. Wehope to have this come out next summer, but it's gonna be about all this, that we've been talking about right now.

Saladino:
The world needs that book, Chris, so godspeed my friend!

References:

Slide 1:
Can linleic acid contribute to coronary artery disease?
Hodgson JM et al.
Am J Clin Nutr. 1993 Aug; 58(2): 228-34

Slide 2:
USDA Economic Research Service, CDC NHANES survey
Prepared by Stephan J. Guyenet

Slide 3:
Graph Courtesy of Catherina Shanahan, MD - Copyright 2020

Slide 4:
Prevalence of weight categories in males - NCDRisC (2017)
OurWorldInData.org/obesity - CC BY

Slide 5:
Prevalence of Obesity in Sweden
Neovius M, Janson A, Rössner A
Obesity Reviews. 7 (1): 1-3

Slide 6:
WHO, Global Health Observatory
OurWorldInData.org/obesity - CC BY

Slide 7:
Keys A.
Atherosclerosis: A problem in newer public
health. *J Mt Sinai Hosp NY.* 1953; 20 (2); 118-
39 nicht auf zlib

Slide 8:
Yerushalmy J, Hilleboe HE
Fat in the diet and mortality from heart disease; a methodologic note
N Y State J Med. 1957 Jul 15; 57 (14): 2343-54

Slide 9:
Adachi H, Asuka H.
Trends in nutritional intake and serum cholesterol levels over 40 years
in Tanushimaru, Japanese men
J Epidemiol. 2005 May; 15 (3): 85-9.

Slide 10:

Minami Y et al.
The Increase of Female Breast Cancer Incidence in Japan: Emergence of Birth Cohort Effect *Int J Cancer.* 2004, 108, 901-906.
Slide 11:
Nobuo Nishi
Monitoring Obesity Trends in Health Japan 21
J Nutr Sci Vitaminol. 2015, 61, S17-S19
Slide 12:
Willcox C et al.
They Really Are That Old: A Validation Study of Centenarian Prevalence in Okinawa
The Journals of Gerontology. 2008, April, Series A, Volume 63, Issue 4, p. 338-349.
Slide 13:
Willcox D et al.
The Okinawan diet: health implications of a low-calorie, nutrient-dense, antioxidant-rich dietary pattern low in glycemic load
J Am Coll Nutr. 2009. Aug, 28 Suppl: S500-S516
Slide 14:
Willcox BJ et al.
Caloric restriction, the traditional Okinawan diet, and healthy aging: the diet of the world's longest-lived people and its potential impact on morbidity and life span
Ann NY Acad Sci. 2007. 1114: 434-455
Slide 15:
Willcox D et al.
The Okinawan diet: health implications of a low-calorie, nutrient-dense, antioxidant-rich dietary pattern low in glycemic load
J Am Coll Nutr. 2009. Aug, 28 Suppl: S500-S516
Slide 16:
Tanaka H, Shimabukuro T, Shimabukuro M
High prevalence of Metabolic Syndrome among men in Okinawa
J Atheroscler Thromb. 2005; 12 (5): 284-8
Slide 17:
Okuyama H et al.
Medicines and Vegetable Oils as Hidden Causes of Cardiovascular Disease and Diabetes
Pharmacology. 2016; 98 (3-4): 134-70
Slide 18:
Gavrilova NS, Gavrilov LA
Comments on Dietary Restriction, Okinawa Diet and Longevity
Gerentology. 2012; 58: 221-223
Slide 19:

Lands WEM
Diets could prevent many diseases
Lipids. 2003, May. 38 (4): 317-21
Slide 20:
Ramsden CE et al.
Lowering dietary linoleic acid reduces bioactive oxidized linoleic acid metabolites in humans
Prostaglandins Leukot Essent Fatty Acids. 2012 October; 87 (4-5): 135-141
Slide 21:
Vallve JA et al.
Unsaturated fatty acids and their oxidation products stimulate CD36 gene expression in human macrophages *Atherosclerosis.* 2002 Sep; 164 (1): 45-56
Slide 22:
Parthasarathy S et al.
Low density lipoprotein rich in oleic acid is protected against oxidative modification: implications for dietary prevention of atherosclerosis
Proc Natl Acad Sci USA. 1990. May; 87 (10): 3894-8
Slide 23:
Turpeinen AM, Basau S, Mutanen M
A high linoleic acid diet increases oxidative stress in vivo and affects oxide metabolism in humans
Prostaglandins Leukot Essent Fatty Acids. 1998 Sep; 59 (3): 229-33
Slide 24:
Silaste ML et al.
Changes in dietary fat intake alter plasma levels of oxidized low-density lipoprotein and lipoprotein(a)
Arterioscler Thromb Vasc Biol. 2004, Mar; 24 (3): 498-503

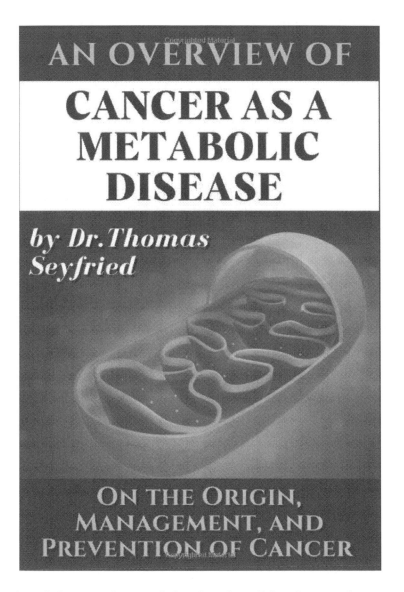

25% of the royalties of this book will be donated to Dr. Seyfrieds research!

<u>This research will actually make a REAL impact, as it studies the real causes and treatment opportunities of cancer!</u>

This book is a summary of Dr. Thomas Seyfrieds book "Cancer as a metabolic disease" and comprises transcripts of his talks and interviews, as well as texts by his collegue Dr. Dominic D'Agostiono and Travis Christofferson (whose foundation will be supported by this book).

Here the original Book description:

The book addresses controversies related to the origins of cancer and provides solutions to cancer management and
prevention. It expands upon Otto Warburg's well-known theory that all cancer is a disease of energy metabolism. However,
Warburg did not link his theory to the "hallmarks of cancer" and thus his theory was discredited.

This book aims to provide evidence, through case studies, that cancer is primarily a metabolic disease requring metabolic solutions for its management and prevention.

Support for this position is derived from critical assessment of current cancer theories. Brain cancer case studies are presented as a proof of principle for metabolic solutions to disease management, but similarities are drawn to other types of cancer, including breast and colon, due to the same cellular mutations that they demonstrate.

The book offers 11 Chapters of revised transcripts of Dr. Jordan Peterson & Mikhaila Peterson on:

- **how they cured their disease, depression and health issues with the carnivore diet and**
- **how ill people could start this kind of eating as well.**

The Transcripts are as follows:

1.   The Agenda with Steve Paikin Digesting Depression
2.   Joe Rogan Podcast 1070
3.   Joe Rogan Podcast 1139
4.   Podcast Interview of Mikhaila Peterson with Robb Wolf, including blood work
5.   Podcast Interview with Ivor Cummins
6.   Talk by Mikhaila Peterson at the Carnivore Conference in Boulder, 2019
7.   Mikhaila Petersons Blog: The Diet Introduction of her Lion Diet on YouTube
8.   Mikhaila Peterson: Should you start an elimination diet?
9.   Mikhaila Peterson: Jordan Peterson's Lion Diet
10 Mikhaila Peterson: The Lion Diet (Introduction of her diet on YouTube

11. Bonus-Transcript: Dr. Shawn Baker talking about his coronary calcium score and overall health status with years of being carnivore.

The transcriptions are revised, which means that the grammar and the wordsequences got corrected, adding phrases here and there, as well as leaving out other elements that hinder understanding and the joy of reading.

Sources

Chapter

1) Text and slides based on Youtube video:

Channel: Paul Saladino, MD

Channel-Url:

https://www.youtube.com/channel/UCgBgoLcHfnJDPmFTTf677Pw

Title: Misinformation: the dangers of banning my post on seed oils

Video-Url: https://www.youtube.com/watch?v=DbPze5Rychc

2) Text and slides based on Youtube video:

Channel: Paul Saladino, MD

Channel-Url: See above

Titel: How seed oils make you fat with Tucker Goodrich and Jeff Nobbs

Video-Url: https://www.youtube.com/watch?v=wrLi4zy9xU

3) Text and slides based on Youtube video:

Channel: Paul Saladino, MD   **Channel-Url: See above Title:** The Omega-6 Apocalypse: are seed oils to blame for diabetes, heart attacks, and chronic disease?

Video-Url: https://www.youtube.com/watch?v=_ZKiq6KC1Ps

Thanks to Dr. Paul Saladino for his important work to cure people of our modern diseases!

His Twitter Account and Instagram:

https://twitter.com/carnivoremd
https://www.insta-gram.com/carnivoremd2.0